HEROES OF HISTORY

GEORGE WASHINGTON

True
Patriot

To Laura, our first American

HEROES OF HISTORY

GEORGE WASHINGTON

True
Patriot

JANET & GEOFF BENGE

Emerald
Books

P.O. BOX 635, LYNNWOOD, WA 98046

Emerald Books are distributed through YWAM Publishing. For a full list of titles, including other great biographies, visit our website at www.ywampublishing.com or call 1-800-922-2143.

Library of Congress Cataloging-in-Publication Data

Benge, Janet, 1958-
    George Washington : true patriot / Janet and Geoff Benge.
        p. cm. -- (Heroes of history)
Includes bibliographical references.
Summary: A biography of George Washington, Commander in Chief of the Continental Army and first president of the United States.
    ISBN 1-883002-81-8
  1. Washington, George, 1732-1799--Juvenile literature. 2. Presidents--United States--Biography--Juvenile literature. 3. Generals--United States--Biography--Juvenile literature. [1. Washington, George, 1732-1799. 2. Presidents.] I. Benge, Geoff, 1954- II. Title.
    E312.66 .B46 2001
    973.4'1'092--dc21

                                        2001006258

Published by Emerald Books
P.O. Box 635
Lynnwood, Washington 98046

ISBN 1-883002-81-8

HEROES OF HISTORY
Biographies

George Washington Carver
Meriwether Lewis
Abraham Lincoln
William Penn
George Washington

More Heroes of History coming soon!
Unit study curriculum guides are available
for these biographies.

Available at your local bookstore or
through Emerald Books
1 (800) 922-2143

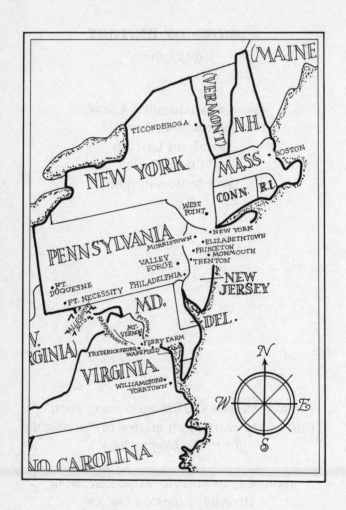

Contents

Contents

Chapter 1

The Enemy

It was July 1775 when George Washington caught his first glimpse of *the enemy*. He stood peering through his spyglass at a battalion of British soldiers. Each soldier was dressed in a bright red coat and buff breeches. In unison the soldiers swung around in drill formation, their muskets gleaming in the morning sun. Behind them were rows of cannons, lined up with military precision. The harbor was thick with British navy ships, their decks scrubbed clean and the Union Jack flying proudly at the top of each vessel's main mast.

For a long time George stood watching, a strange swirl of emotions playing in his head. There was no denying it was a glorious sight. He couldn't help but admire the British troops. Indeed, the British had not always been the enemy. George had been born a British subject, as had everyone born in the thirteen American colonies. His older half brother had fought for the English against the Spanish. And Mount Vernon, George's plantation in Virginia, was named after a British admiral.

George himself had once set his heart on being an officer in the British army. He had been a part of General Braddock's force when the British struggled with the French and Indians for control of the territory beyond the western boundaries of the colonies. Serving under General Braddock, George had found a grit and determination he did not know he possessed and a flare for leading men into battle. And now he was going to use everything General Braddock had taught him about waging war to fight against the army he had once served with. George Washington was now a patriot. He was one of the upstart colonists who were determined to drive the British out of the colonies.

George's mother was not in favor of the undertaking. She thought the patriots could never organize themselves enough to fight the world's most powerful army. Maybe she was right. But there was no going back for George now. The stakes were too high. If the patriots had misjudged the number of colonists who would join their cause or the determination of the British to hold on to their American colonies, they would lose the fight. If that happened, most of the ragtag band of patriot soldiers who had gathered to fight could go home again but not George Washington. He was commander in chief of the new Continental army. If he did not drive the British from North America, there was only one outcome for him—the British would hang him as a traitor.

But then, the little boy born February 22, 1732, in the tidewater area of Virginia had a knack for making it against the odds. And George was almost certain as he peered across Boston Harbor through his spyglass that he could defeat the very army he once desperately wanted to be a part of.

...and one drew the United States from North America. There was only one outcome for him: that of a citizen of the United States as a whole.

That there, on that black bay area between 22 and 27...

in the tidewater area of Virginia he assembled for...

that, although that the whole circumstance was through...

great... happened across Boston... father through...

his symbols... that he could defend the very army he...

made Bay... only wanted to be a part of...

Chapter 2

Big Brother

Six-year-old George Washington climbed his favorite oak tree and scanned the horizon. He could see the swirling waters of Little Hunting Creek emptying into the mile-wide Potomac River. Four ships, majestic with their sails billowing in the stiff breeze, maneuvered their way along the river. George knew the ships had come from England, across the Atlantic Ocean, through Chesapeake Bay, and on up the Potomac. And now, as they sailed past Epsewasson, George could make out sailors standing on their aft decks. A thrill ran through him as he asked himself the same question he had asked a thousand times before: Was Lawrence aboard one of the ships?

George hoped his twenty-year-old half brother was aboard one of the vessels. He was tired of waiting for Lawrence to arrive from England. Of course he had never met Lawrence or his other half brother, Austin, but he felt as though he already knew them. His father often told him that Lawrence was tall and fair like George and was very well mannered. Lawrence had also done well at Appleby School in Westmoreland, England, which he had attended since he was twelve years old. George had so many questions to ask Lawrence, especially about Appleby School. When George turned twelve, he would be attending there himself, though that would not be until 1744, six long years away.

"Ma says to get down and come inside before you break your neck. Besides, can't you see those black clouds? You know what that means," came a little voice from the base of the tree.

George sighed. It was his bossy little sister Betty.

"Me too. Up. Up!" exclaimed another voice.

George looked down to see his two-year-old brother, Jack, with his arms outstretched. "Not right now, Jack," George said. "It's going to rain, and Ma always wants us inside before it rains."

George slipped down out of the tree and took Jack by the hand. The three children hurried toward Epsewasson's main farmhouse. George could see his four-year-old brother, Samuel, and his mother standing on the wide front porch. His mother was holding Charles, George's newborn brother, in her arms as she peered anxiously at the darkening sky.

"I wish your father were home," she wailed as she hustled the children indoors. "Stay away from the chimney, everyone. George, make your brothers and sister sit still."

George obediently sat his sister and younger brothers in a circle, just as he always did when a storm was brewing. He knew his mother was deathly afraid of storms, and who could blame her? Everyone within fifty miles of Epsewasson knew the terrible story. Several years before, when the Washingtons lived forty miles away on Wakefield farm on Pope's Creek, a tributary of the Potomac River, George's mother had invited a neighboring family to Sunday dinner. As they all sat down to eat, a storm rolled in. Thunder rumbled and lightning crackled through the air. One bolt of lightning hit the farmhouse and traveled down the chimney, across the floor, and up the leg of a chair on which a twelve-year-old girl sat. The power of the strike not only killed the girl but also fused together the metal knife and fork she was holding.

Mrs. Washington had told George the story many times to warn him about the dangers of lightning and any other dangers she could imagine. George found it very difficult to have the kind of adventures he longed for while under the constant supervision of his overcautious mother, not to mention always having two little brothers and an eagle-eyed sister in tow.

The first peals of thunder crashed, and Mrs. Washington grabbed Charles and clasped him to her chest. As the infant whimpered, George listened carefully. Was there another noise? Could he hear the rumbling of horses' hooves? He cocked his head and listened some more.

Suddenly the door burst open. Filling the doorway was George's father accompanied by another man—a young man. George's eyes grew wide with excitement. Was this his brother Lawrence?

"Gus, you shouldn't have been out in the storm," George's mother scolded, then stopped short. "Lawrence?" she asked.

Mr. Washington slapped the tall young man on the back. "Come in and meet your family," he said.

Soon the three adults were drinking tea and eating scones. George and his younger siblings sat still and listened to their conversation. Most of all, though, George just stared at his half brother.

Lawrence was George's father's oldest son by his first wife. After she had died, George's father had married George's mother. Lawrence was tall and fair like their father, though as Mrs. Washington pointed out when she offered him another scone, he was quite thin.

Lawrence laughed. "It wasn't an easy voyage," he said. "Sixty days to cross the Atlantic Ocean, and not one of them calm. No wonder I lost weight."

George tried to take in every detail about this brother he had never met before. Lawrence had an oval, friendly face with a dimple in his chin and blue eyes just like George and Betty. He wore a fine white linen shirt and a green velvet vest with shiny gold buttons. He held the knife delicately in his hand as he buttered his scone, and he never spoke with his mouth full. This was something George's mother had been nagging George about with little success.

When the adults finished their tea and scones, one of the slaves came in with two leather bags. Another two slaves appeared carrying a trunk between them. "Where do you want this, master?" one of them asked.

George's father pointed to a spot beside the table. "There will be fine," he said.

Soon the trunk and bags were opened. It was better than Christmas! Lawrence pulled out silk fabric and boxes of Indian tea for his stepmother, a folding card table and ivory chess set for his father, and even a present for each of the children. George got a toy gun, not a crude wooden one like his cousins played with, but a heavy gun made of lead. It was better than anything he had ever imagined. From then on, Lawrence was George's hero.

George wished he could spend every day with his new big brother, but Lawrence had many more important things to do. Mr. Washington had many projects going at once, and he needed his oldest son to take over some of them. Lawrence learned how to manage the iron mining works and furnace that his father owned at Accokeek Creek.

After several months Mr. Washington decided it was time to give Lawrence some responsibility of his own. Lawrence would manage Epsewasson farm while the rest of George's family moved to a farm on the west bank of the Rappahannock River opposite the town of Fredericksburg, Virginia. The farm was within easy riding distance of the iron-works, which George's father hoped to make more profitable. Mr. Washington bought 260 acres of land, along with a wooden six-room farmhouse, and leased another 300 acres. Much of the land had never been plowed before, and George's father intended to grow tobacco once the slaves had broken it in.

The day George found out about the move was not a happy one for him. He had grown very attached to his older brother and dreaded being stuck in the house with the younger children all the time. Still, there was nothing he could do about it, and he even had to admit to a twinge of excitement as all of the family's possessions were loaded into huge barrels and rolled down to the dock. There the barrels were arranged on a barge for the trip to Ferry Farm, as the new farm was called. Ferry Farm had a dock right on the property where people gathered to wait for the ferry to cross the river to Fredericksburg.

Finally everything was ready for the voyage. The last of the chickens, calves, and piglets let out squeals and squawks of protest as their legs were tied together and they were carried on board. The family set off downriver, slaves poling the barges while Mr. Washington stood at the front of the lead barge and yelled instructions on how to avoid the overhanging tree limbs and eddies in the river.

As much as George missed his older brother Lawrence, he soon found that the new farm had some great advantages. He loved to stand at his bedroom window or down by the ferry dock and gaze across the river to Fredericksburg. He had never before seen a town like Fredericksburg, which always seemed to be bustling with people. He also loved to watch as goods such as wood, rice, indigo dyes, tobacco, and animal furs were loaded on to barges to be taken downriver to be loaded onto ships bound for England. The barges would return upriver laden with clothing, glass, clocks, books, kettles, and carpenters' tools from England.

As he watched the barges being loaded and unloaded, George could hardly wait until the time when he would be climbing aboard a ship and setting sail for England to attend school. How different that would be from Ferry Farm and Fredericksburg. But before George would be ready for school in England, he needed to learn to read, write, and do math. So when he was seven years old, his parents decided he was ready to start learning. George's mother taught him the basics of reading and writing and how to add and subtract numbers. After this George began attending a small school in Fredericksburg, where he enjoyed learning how to draw maps most of all.

To help him improve his penmanship, tutors at the school had George copy out page after page from a book called *Rules of Civility and Decent Behavior in Company and Conversation*. Once George would have laughed at the rules in this book, but since meeting Lawrence he was eager to

learn all he could about being a proper English gentleman. George memorized many of the rules and
recited them as he went to sleep at night, especially
the ones he knew he had to work on the most.

When he was not studying, George loved to ride
his horse around the farm. Since his father was a
very busy man, with several farms and the iron-
works and furnace to take care of, his mother had
taught him to ride. Actually, she was one of the
best riders in the district, and since every Virginia
gentleman rode a horse, she was determined to
teach George the safest way to mount a horse and
get it cantering.

George was an eager pupil, and by the time he
was eight years old, he was galloping over the hills
delivering messages for his father. And although
his mother forbade him to ride all the way to
Epsewasson, much to George's relief Lawrence visited Ferry Farm whenever he could. On these visits
Mr. Washington and Lawrence would discuss the
price that tobacco was fetching in England and
how much iron ore the mine was producing. When
Lawrence was finished with such discussions, he
would go riding with George. As they rode,
Lawrence would tell George about all he had done
since his last visit.

On one of these rides Lawrence had exciting
news for George. A week before, the *Virginia
Gazette* had reported that British Admiral Edward
Vernon was fighting a war with Spain in the Gulf of
Darien, at the southern end of the Caribbean Sea.
For the first time ever, Britain was asking the

American colonies to raise an army for an overseas expedition to help the British attack various Spanish forts along the Colombian coast. "Just think," Lawrence said, "they need three thousand men from the thirteen colonies, four hundred of whom are to come from Virginia. And Governor Gooch gets to appoint four captains for the Virginia Regiment. I intend to be one of those four!"

"Really, Lawrence? Are you really going to be a captain?" George asked excitedly.

"I'm certainly going to try," Lawrence replied. "The home country needs us, and frankly, I find plantation life a little dull, don't you?"

George laughed. No wonder he liked his half brother so much. Lawrence had the same quest for adventure flowing through his veins as George did.

The following week George saw evidence of the war for himself. He was walking from his schoolhouse down to the water's edge when he heard music. He swung around and headed back toward the main street, where he saw the most fantastic sight: rows of soldiers clad in red coats and buff breeches were marching down the street. Some played fifes while others twilled on drums and waved the British flag.

"What are they doing?" George asked a man who was standing outside the general store.

"That's the British army, lad. They're recruiting young men for Admiral Vernon's war."

George's chest swelled with pride. "Well, sir," George replied, "I already know one soldier who is going. My big brother Lawrence!"

The man smiled down at George and ruffled George's reddish blond hair.

A week later Lawrence Washington burst through the door at Ferry Farm. He was wearing a bright red uniform with gold-trimmed lapels, and a crimson sash draped across his shoulder held a silver short sword. But best of all was the gorget that hung like a necklace around his neck. A gorget was a crescent-shaped piece of beaten brass, the badge of a military officer!

George rushed over to examine his brother's uniform. "When will you sail?" he asked.

"Probably in October," Lawrence replied, "though I have a lot to do before then."

Soon the whole family was clustered around Lawrence, eager to hear every bit of information he had about his appointment. He hadn't been told much. The governor told them they would get their instructions from the British when they got to the Caribbean.

George was allowed to take the day off from school when Lawrence set sail for the Caribbean aboard a British transport ship. All of the family was there to see him off, except Mrs. Washington, who was at home caring for the latest addition to the Washington family, a baby daughter named Mildred, who was very sick.

Soon after Lawrence sailed away, Mildred died. It was sad but not unexpected news for the family. In fact, George knew they were luckier than a lot of families. Most of his friends at school had lost at least three or four brothers and sisters, children who had died young, usually from various diseases.

Mrs. Washington was sad for a long time, and George was glad he was old enough to escape into the woods with his rifle. It was such an adventure out there. He never knew what he would spot—a fox, an elk, a hare, even a bear! Most of all, though, George liked the challenge of stalking white-tailed deer. As he stalked the animal, he imagined he was Lawrence creeping up on a Spanish soldier, slowly getting closer, then stopping, aiming his rifle at the target, and gently squeezing the trigger. Bang! The deer would fall to the ground dead. It was always a proud moment for George when the dead animal was butchered and cooked and served up for the family to eat.

A year went by without any word from Lawrence. Occasionally someone heard a rumor of what was happening in the Caribbean. Someone even said that nearly all of the Virginia Regiment had been wiped out in a battle, but no one knew for sure. Then one day in October 1742, two years after Lawrence had left, a battered troop ship flying the British flag arrived in Virginia.

George's heart pounded when he learned it was one of Admiral Vernon's ships. Was Lawrence on board? The question burned in George's mind as he ran home to tell his mother the news of the ship's arrival.

Chapter 3

Changes

"A ustin, Austin!" George called after he had delivered the good news about the ship to his mother. Austin was George's other half brother. He had recently returned to Virginia from school in England, and George was eager for him to hear the news, too. "A British warship has arrived in Virginia from the Caribbean, and I bet Lawrence is on board!" he blurted out.

"I hope you're right," Austin replied, looking up from the papers he was sorting through. "If he is on the ship, I'm sure it will be only a matter of days before he arrives here at the farm."

Two days passed, and George waited anxiously to see if Lawrence would come. Then late one afternoon, as the sun cast long shadows across the ground, George spotted a man clothed in a faded red uniform approaching Ferry Farm on horse-back. "Lawrence," he yelled at the top of his lungs as he ran toward the horse. His big brother was home at last!

It was a wonderful reunion for the family. Mrs. Washington prepared a feast for dinner. The best silver and china were laid out as the family sat down to dine on platters of fish, chicken, oysters, and roast pork shoulder. As they ate, Lawrence told them stories about the war. Some of them were funny, like the one about the extra-stiff coat Admiral Vernon insisted on wearing all the time. The coat was made of grogram, a coarse fabric, and the American soldiers soon nicknamed him "Old Grog." When the rations of rum began to run low, "Old Grog" Vernon mixed the liquor with water, and soon the diluted drink was known simply as "grog."

Lawrence sounded angry, though, when he told stories about the way British commanders treated some of the American regiments. The Americans were often ordered to do the most dangerous jobs, such as dragging ladders up to the walls of forts so that British soldiers could scale them. Most of the men putting the ladders in place were gunned down. When one American soldier was killed, another was expected to run out and take his place.

The men had had other enemies to face besides the Spaniards. Diseases like scurvy, dysentery, yellow fever, and malaria took their toll on the soldiers. George heard Lawrence tell their father in a low voice that of the 400 men who had set out from

Virginia, fewer than 120 had survived. The rest were buried at sea or on the battlefield. But even sober news like this did not stop the family festivities. Everyone was glad to have Lawrence safely home.

The following day George and Lawrence mounted their horses and galloped over to Epsewasson.

"I'm going to rename the farm," Lawrence confided in his younger half brother. "From now on it's going to be called Mount Vernon, after the admiral."

It sounded like a great idea to George, who thought the British admiral deserved to have things named after him, even if he did wear a stiff coat.

"Wait until you see what's been built next door," George told his brother as they neared the plantation. "It's got to be the grandest house in the county."

Lawrence whistled when he finally caught a glimpse of the brick mansion.

"It's called Belvoir, and Colonel William Fairfax from Massachusetts built it. His cousin is Lord Fairfax, who lives in England. Colonel Fairfax is in charge of his cousin's affairs in the colonies," George said, proud that he had some information to impress his brother with. "And I haven't seen her yet, but they say he has a very pretty daughter named Anne."

Lawrence laughed. "You must have been talking to your mother. She's already trying to marry me off, and I haven't been home more than twenty-four hours."

George and Lawrence spent a happy day riding all over newly named Mount Vernon and talking to the manager, who had been in charge while Lawrence was away. Lawrence was not impressed with the job the manager had done and wanted to move back into the farmhouse as soon as possible.

George's other half brother, Austin, moved to Wakefield Farm, located on Pope's Creek, a tributary of the Potomac River. By Christmas George had two farms to escape to when he'd had enough of his mother's overbearing ways. He also had lots of studying to do so that he would be ready for school in England.

At Easter 1743 eleven-year-old George was allowed to visit his cousins who lived at Chotank, also located on Pope's Creek. He had been there only a couple of days when a message arrived from his mother telling him his father was sick and that George should hurry home. George raced back to Ferry Farm, convinced that his father was going to die. He was right. Soon after George arrived home, Augustine Washington died at forty-nine years of age.

The funeral was a sober affair, with George reading the prayers at Bridges Creek Cemetery, where his father was buried. After the service was over, George wandered among the tombstones. Buried next to his father were his grandfather, Lawrence Washington, and great-grandfather, John Washington, who had come to Virginia from England.

Three weeks after the funeral the family gathered at the courthouse in Fredericksburg for the reading of the will. The complicated document strove to be fair at a time when many fathers left everything they owned to their oldest son. Everybody got some property. Lawrence inherited Mount Vernon; Austin, Wakefield; and George, Ferry Farm. There was just one catch for George: his mother got to run the farm until he was twenty-one years old. George also inherited three lots in Fredericksburg, a fifth of his father's personal property, twenty-one hundred acres of undeveloped land, and ten slaves.

It was all a bit much for George to take in. He would gladly have swapped it all to have his father back again, especially when he found out what his mother had in store for him. With the death of his father, George lost all hope of going to England to get an education. His mother would not hear of it.

"What if you are shipwrecked on the way?" she asked. "Or you fall into bad company at school? And what about your brothers and sister? They need a man about the house. You need to be that man."

George pleaded with his mother to change her mind. Lawrence and Austin offered to help out at Ferry Farm while he was gone, but nothing worked. Once Mary Washington had made up her mind, there was no changing it, no matter what.

It was a bitter disappointment for George. At eleven years of age he did not want to assume the role of second father that his mother thrust on him. But there was nothing he could do about it except to escape whenever he could.

Lawrence and George thought up all sorts of excuses for George to visit Mount Vernon. In the

meantime Lawrence had indeed made the acquaintance of Miss Anne Fairfax, and before long they
were in a whirlwind romance. They were married
two months after Mr. Washington died, and Anne
proved to be a kind and generous sister-in-law to
George.

Although he would never have confessed it to
anyone, George was in awe of the Fairfax family.
Belvoir was the grandest house he had ever been
in. It had two sitting rooms and enough silver to
serve twenty people at a dinner party. Soon George
was being invited along to dinner parties there,
and he made it a practice never to say much. He
kept his mouth tightly shut and instead watched
the way fancy people spoke and acted. Sometimes
as he watched, he would recite some of the 110
rules of civility to himself. "Rule 40: Strive not with
your superiors in argument, but always submit
your judgment to others with modesty." "Rule 73:
Think before you speak. Pronounce not imperfectly
nor bring out your words too hastily but orderly
and distinctly."

By the time he was fourteen, George was spending most weekends and all of his vacations with
Lawrence and Anne. Together the three of them
worked out ways to get around the bleak life Mary
Washington had mapped out for her oldest son.

Lawrence, who had recently been elected to the
Virginia House of Burgesses, encouraged George to
consider a career in the British Royal Navy. This
would not be easy, but with a little maneuvering,
everyone felt that Mrs. Washington would agree in

the end. George also started to take fencing and wrestling lessons, both of which Lawrence paid for. Finally, Colonel Fairfax offered to help him get a job aboard a British naval ship as a midshipman. Once everything was arranged, George had only one job left to do: tell his mother he was leaving.

It was a scene George would never forget. He waited until the younger children were all in bed before he told his mother of his plans. She yelled and cried, pleaded, and then absolutely forbade him to leave the farm. He had a duty there, she warned him, a lifelong duty.

It felt more like a life sentence than a duty to George. But he knew he was beaten. The ship would have to sail without him. He and Colonel Fairfax and his brother Lawrence were no match for Mary Washington when she had made up her mind.

While George's career at sea was as dead as his previous hopes of going to school in England, he would not give up. He had inherited his mother's stubbornness, and somehow he was going to find a way to break free and enjoy adventures of his own.

It took him two more years to work out a way to have such adventures, and in those two years two new people moved to the Belvoir estate next door to Mount Vernon. The first was George Fairfax, the colonel's son and Anne's younger brother. He arrived from England, where he'd spent fifteen years being educated. The two Georges quickly became friends, even though George Fairfax was seven years older and used to a much different life in England. Still, he was in the colonies now, and as he explained to George Washington, certain allowances had to be made. The two of them loved to ride horses over the vast tracts of land that belonged to Lord Fairfax.

Then, in 1747, Lord Fairfax himself arrived in Virginia. He was a grumpy man who barked out orders, hated women, and loved fox hunting. It did not take him long to realize that George Washington was the best rider in the area. As a result, he often invited George to go along on fox hunts. Of course George had to make sure he never got to the fox ahead of Lord Fairfax. A man that rich and powerful did not like to be shown up!

Soon George became a familiar sight around Belvoir. Everyone liked him, and he used the opportunity to study how important people acted and talked. He also constantly borrowed books to read for his self-improvement.

George was doing something else, too—a hobby, really. In the shed behind the house at Ferry Farm, George had discovered his father's old surveying equipment. Since he loved mathematics, he decided to teach himself how to use the tools. He figured out from a book what to do, and soon he had surveyed Lawrence's turnip patch. He then plotted the boundary line between Mount Vernon and Belvoir.

It was these three events—the arrivals of George Fairfax and Lord Fairfax and teaching himself to survey—that worked together to change the course of George Washington's life. The adventure he craved was just around the corner.

Chapter 4

The Young Surveyor

Join the surveying team? Had George heard right? Was Colonel Fairfax suggesting that he be part of the team that would cross the Blue Ridge Mountains and map out the Fairfax land in the Shenandoah Valley?

"I think it would be good for you to go along," Colonel Fairfax said, taking a puff of his cigar. "I am sending my son George along as the family representative, and he'd like to have some company. I hear you know a little about surveying yourself, so you can try your hand at it if you like. In fact, if you are willing to be the chainman for James Genn, I think I can even give you a small salary."

George took a deep breath. This was just what he wanted—the opportunity to do something new and different. But one question lurked in the back of his mind: Would his mother let him go? After all, he would be crossing the mountains and entering the western frontier, where Indians and trappers roamed. However, George thought his mother might agree to his going because of one thing—the money. George would be getting paid for his labor. Mrs. Washington constantly complained about how much money it cost to raise the children, while at the same time she allowed Ferry Farm to run down to the point where it made only half as much money from tobacco as it had when George's father was alive. There was little George or Lawrence could do about this. Mary Washington had a firm grip on Ferry Farm. Indeed, as time passed, it had become obvious to George that his mother had no intention of leaving the farm when he turned twenty-one.

George was right, and Mary Washington did agree to his taking the surveying job. She did not consider venturing inland as dangerous as sailing the ocean.

Early on March 11, 1748, less than a month after his sixteenth birthday, George Washington mounted his horse and headed west. Twenty-three-year-old George Fairfax rode beside him. By midafternoon the horses were making their way over the hard-packed snow of Dumries Road. "It's a good thing spring is late this year," George remarked as they rode. "It's much easier to survey when the trees have no leaves. Otherwise we'd have to cut them down to get clear sightings."

George smiled to himself as the young English-man, George Fairfax, gulped. Finally George

Washington was in a situation where he had the advantage. He was over six feet tall now, with a strong back and large hands. In contrast, George Fairfax was short, with milky skin and an aversion to getting his fashionable English clothes dirty.

By nightfall the pair had covered forty miles and reached Neville's tavern, where they met up with James Genn and the rest of the survey party. Two days later they passed through Ashby's Gap and into the first block of Lord Fairfax's land. They toiled hard all day. George scurried about, dragging the thirty-three-foot-long chain with eight-inch links, or carried from place to place the heavy tripod that held the circumferentor. James Genn used the circumferentor to measure off the land.

Finally night came, and the men hungrily gulped down their dinner. The inns they slept in were becoming more primitive the farther west they went. In one of these inns George naively stripped off his clothes and lay down on the thin mattress. Since there were no sheets, he pulled the thread-bare blanket over him. This was a big mistake. Instantly lice, fleas, and ticks assailed him. While the fleas bit him, the ticks burrowed under his skin. George leapt up and brushed the attackers off. He put all his clothes back on, left the blanket and mattress where they were, and lay down on the packed-mud floor. The floor was hard and uncomfortable, and in the morning George was stiff.

Over the next several days the survey party pushed farther into the wilderness. They swam their horses across swollen rivers, canoed up creeks, and chopped down huge trees that stood in the way of their surveying efforts. On the eleventh day a group of thirty Indians whooped into camp. They were friendly enough, though disappointed. They were returning from a raid on another tribe and had only one scalp to show for their efforts. Still, with a little rum to persuade them, the Indians agreed to perform a war dance for the survey party.

George Washington found the whole affair fascinating. He'd seen the occasional Indian around Fredericksburg, but he had never been in the midst of a large group of them. That night he wrote in his journal:

> We had a war dance. Their manner of dancing is as follows: They clear a large circle and make a great fire in the middle, then seat themselves around it. The speaker makes a grand speech...[then] the best dancer jumps up as one awaked out of a sleep and runs and jumps about the ring in a most comical manner. He is followed by the rest. Then begins their musicians to play the music. There is a pot half full of water with a deerskin stretched over it as tight as it can and a gourd with some shot in it to rattle and a piece of a horse's tail tied to it to make it look fine. The one keeps rattling and the other drumming, all the while the others are dancing.

It started to rain the next day, and it didn't stop for a week. George Fairfax soon got tired of being wet all day and gave up the surveying life. He found a comfortable inn and waited for George Washington and the rest of the surveyors to complete their work. It was a month before everything was done to James Genn's satisfaction, and the men were dismissed to find their own way home.

The month away changed George Washington. For one thing, he had grown up. He had been doing a man's job for a man's wages, and he had done it well. For another thing, he had discovered a way to get out from under his mother's grip. James Genn was impressed with George's surveying ability and urged George to study for his surveyor's license. With this license George could go into business for himself, and with the Fairfax land being opened up, there was plenty of surveying work for everyone.

With money jangling in his pocket, George rode home, not to stay but to prepare himself for a life as a surveyor. At the same time George Fairfax was embarking on quite a different life. He became engaged to Sally Cary, a dark-haired eighteen-year-old from a wealthy family. George Washington spent some of his money on dancing lessons so that he would not make a fool of himself at George Fairfax's upcoming wedding.

In early July 1749 seventeen-year-old George Washington earned his ticket to freedom—a surveyor's license. Two days later he had his first assignment, mapping out more of Lord Fairfax's land in the Shenandoah Valley. Soon he was also appointed county surveyor of Culpepper County, with a base salary of fifteen pounds, plus any fees he charged. By the end of his first year George had earned 125 pounds. This was a good sum of money, enough to buy a new pocket watch, fine linen shirts and waistcoats, and a 450-acre parcel of land in the Shenandoah Valley.

George wore his new clothes to his sister Betty's wedding. At sixteen she married Fielding Lewis, a rich widower who had one child. It seemed a happy enough match, and George wished he himself could find someone to marry, but he was too shy to make small talk, and that's what young women seemed to want.

The next year went equally well for George, and he bought more land. The future looked bright, and even without the land his father had left him, George began to think he could have both adventure and riches.

Life was not going nearly as well for Lawrence. In the five years he and Anne had been married, she had given birth to three children, but they had all died before they could walk. And now it was Lawrence himself who was sick. He had tuberculosis, a dreaded and deadly disease of the lungs.

George watched helplessly as Anne applied different poultices to Lawrence's chest and plied him with herbal concoctions. None of it made any difference, and by the summer of 1751 Lawrence was convinced he would die if he spent another winter in cold, damp Virginia.

A friend of Lord Fairfax recommended that Lawrence visit a doctor he knew in Barbados. The climate there would be warmer, and the doctor had a reputation for being able to cure the disease. Lawrence made up his mind to go, but he was not strong enough to go alone. However, Anne had given birth to another baby, whom they named Sarah. Anne was trying desperately to protect her new daughter from childhood diseases, and taking the child to the tropics was out of the question. As a result George volunteered to accompany his half brother to Barbados.

The two men booked passage to Bridgetown, Barbados, aboard the *Success*. They set sail on September 28, 1751. As a young boy, George had spent many hours watching the sailing ships on the river, imagining how exciting it would be to be aboard one of the vessels. Now, as the wind billowed the sails and the *Success* made its way out into the Atlantic Ocean, George soon began to appreciate his mother's forbidding him to join the navy. He felt sick even before the ship left port and was soon confined to his bunk when the Atlantic swells began to surge around the ship.

Neither George nor Lawrence went above deck for the first ten days of the thirty-seven-day voyage south. Finally, much to George's relief, the *Success* sailed past Fort James and into Bridgetown Harbor. The Washington brothers were welcomed ashore by James Carter, chief justice of Barbados and a good friend of Lord Fairfax.

The next day, George helped Lawrence find his way to Dr. Hilary's office. After examining Lawrence, Dr. Hilary declared that Lawrence's tuberculosis was still in an early stage and could be treated and cured. This was just what George and Lawrence wanted to hear. They set about finding a house so they could settle down and Lawrence could begin treatment.

Everything about the tropical island enchanted George. He tasted avocados and pineapples for the first time. He studied the lush plants and watched dolphins playing in the harbor. And because of the Fairfax connection, George received more invitations to balls, concerts, and parties than he had time to accept. That was for the first two weeks of his stay. Then on Wednesday morning, November 17, George awoke feeling stiff and sore. He tried to get up, but the room swirled around him. He flopped back onto his bed and waited to see what would happen next. As he suspected, red spots began to appear on his skin. George Washington had smallpox!

There was little the doctor could do except give George quinine for the fever. George would either live or die, and chances were strong it would be the latter. However, after twelve days of a soaring temperature and hallucinations, George's mind began to clear—at about the same time his body began to itch unbearably. George scratched the healing scabs furiously in search of relief, not caring if the scratching left pockmarks on his skin.

Finally George was able to get up and walk around again. While George had been sick, Lawrence had continued his tuberculosis treatment, though he became very depressed when it did not appear to be doing much good. In this lonely and discouraged state he urged George to return to Virginia to see how Anne was faring. Lawrence planned to stay on in Barbados or move to Bermuda if his condition got any worse.

George hated to go, first, because he didn't want to leave his brother, and second, because it meant a dreaded sea voyage back. However, Lawrence insisted that he could look after himself and that he really wanted George to return to Virginia to watch over his family.

The *Industry* set sail from Barbados on December 21, 1751, bound for Yorktown, Virginia. The trip back was even worse than the trip down, and by the time George set foot back on Virginia soil, he had vowed never to go to sea again.

In Yorktown he hired a horse and rode to Williamsburg, where he delivered a pouch of official letters from the governor of Barbados to Robert Dinwiddie, Royal Governor of Virginia. Governor Dinwiddie invited George to stay for dinner. As they ate they talked about Barbados and the events that had happened in Virginia during the five months George had been away. It was a pleasant conversation, and although George knew the governor wielded great power, he had no idea the governor was about to use that power to change George's life.

Chapter 5

Major Washington

After returning from Barbados, George went back to his surveying work. The following spring he received a letter from Lawrence that said, "The unhappy state of health which I labor under makes me uncertain as to my return. If I grow worse I shall hurry home to my grave; if better, I shall be induced to stay here longer to complete a cure."

Lawrence Washington arrived back at Mount Vernon in June 1752 and set straight about writing a will. George was constantly at his side, but no amount of care or nursing could help. Lawrence was obviously dying, and on July 26 he took his last breath. George was left to attend another Washington funeral, though this one was even more difficult for him than his father's funeral. George and Lawrence had become very close over the years.

Two weeks after the funeral the will was read. It was a complicated document that left different property to various people, depending upon who died first. Basically, Lawrence left half of everything to his daughter Sarah, while the other half was to be used by Anne for as long as she lived. If Anne died, Sarah would receive her share as well. But if Sarah died before Anne, her half would be split equally among Austin, George, and his three younger brothers. As if that were not difficult enough to work out, if Sarah did die before her mother, when Anne died, her share of the property, including Mount Vernon, would go to George.

There were slaves and other property to be divided up as well, but George soon found that his brother was not nearly as rich as he had once been. Lawrence had been away from the plantation for too long, and in his absence it had not been run efficiently. Besides this, his travel and medical bills had mounted up. Most of Lawrence's personal belongings had to be auctioned off to pay the bills.

George, though, had his eyes firmly on something his brother had but could not pass on in a will—his position as adjunct of the Virginia colony and the red uniform that went with it. The naming of a new adjunct fell to Governor Dinwiddie, whom George had enjoyed dinner with several months before. Immediately George packed his most fashionable clothes and set out for Williamsburg to ask the governor for his late brother's appointment. It was a bold move. George was only twenty years old, and unlike Lawrence he had no military experience. What he did have was connections to the Fairfax family and a lot of ambition.

In the end George got part, though not all, of what he sought. The governor and the Council of Virginia decided to split Virginia into four districts and appointed four adjuncts to replace Lawrence Washington. George was made adjunct over the smallest and least populated of these districts. The district was located at the southern end of the colony between the James River and the border with North Carolina. Most of the land there was swampy, making it an undesirable place for people to settle or fight over.

It wasn't what George had hoped for, but it was a beginning, and it gave him a new rank, that of major. After his appointment George Washington went to Mount Vernon to study Lawrence's books on drilling soldiers and strategies for battle.

Six months after Lawrence's death, Anne remarried and moved to her new husband's plantation. George then moved back to Ferry Farm to live with his mother. In a month or so the farm would be legally his, though his mother was still in firm control of it and had no intention of moving out. So George kept busy surveying and waited for an opportunity to make his mark as a military officer.

Nine months passed before this opportunity presented itself. In late October 1753 George hurried back from a visit at Belvoir. His brother Jack met him at the door. "Will you come and look at one of the pigs? I think it's sick," Jack said.

George strode into the house. "I don't have time, Jack. I'm on my way to Williamsburg."

"What for?" wide-eyed Jack asked.

"I'm going to ask Governor Dinwiddie to send me on a special mission to deliver a message to the French at one of their big forts," George said.

Jack looked puzzled.

George sighed. It was a complicated situation, so complicated that neither he nor anyone else in the colonies for that matter fully understood the situation. Still, Lawrence had taken time to explain things to George when he was younger, and now it was George's turn to do the same for Jack.

"It's like this," George began. "For the past seventy years or so the French and English have been fighting over who owns the lands west of the mountains. The French occupy most of this land right now. In fact, they have forts and trading posts all the way from Quebec to New Orleans. But the British have the real right to the land. The French are not settlers like the English colonists. They come and shoot animals, trade fur with the Indians, and then go home again. The English, people like us, our ancestors, came to settle in America and make a new life for themselves and their families."

"So?" Jack asked, obviously not getting the connection George was trying to make.

"Well, more and more people, and not just the English, are now coming to the British colonies. The French have only about eighty thousand people living in all of New France, but we have over one million people in our colonies. So we're moving through the Cumberland Gap and into the western lands. Traders and hunters are pressing even farther inland."

"The French won't like that!" Jack exclaimed.

George laughed. "You're right about that. Lord Fairfax tells me they've sent fifteen hundred French soldiers to Fort le Boeuf on the shores of Lake Erie. Their job is to arrest all the British traders in the area and ship them back to France for trial and punishment. Someone has to carry a message to the French commander at Fort le Boeuf telling him the land belongs to England and to withdraw his troops. Otherwise we redcoats are prepared to go to war. And that's where I come in. I've decided I'm going to deliver the message!"

"It sounds like a dangerous mission," Jack said, picking up his brother's sword and turning it over in his hands.

"Yes," George said, "but I think I'm the man for the job. After all, I'm the only adjunct who has ridden over the Blue Ridge Mountains, and I'm used to camping out in the wilderness. It would be quite a rude shock for the other gentlemen!"

"Can I come with you if you get the job?" Jack asked.

George shook his head. "You know how Mother is. I'm over twenty-one years old now, and she would forbid me from going if she could."

Jack looked at his big brother glumly and nodded.

A month and a half later, on December 11, 1753, Major George Washington was dining with

Commander St. Pierre at Fort le Boeuf. It had taken
George and his party of trappers, hunters, and
translators six weeks to get there—forty-two days of
slogging through icy rain and snow, sometimes
along nonexistent trails. George had changed into
his Virginia militia dress uniform for the evening.
As St. Pierre poured a glass of wine for his guest,
George noticed the smile playing around his lips.
He knew the commander found it amusing that the
British government had sent such a young, inexpe-
rienced soldier to deliver the message.

St. Pierre then told George that he would have a
reply ready by the following evening, but he already
knew what he would write. He told George that it
was absurd to think the French would give up their
hold over the Ohio Valley. They would fight for what
was rightfully theirs if they had to.

The next day Commander St. Pierre held a meeting of his officers. This gave George an opportunity
to spy on the fort. He counted the number of soldiers and made sketches of the buildings and cannon positions. He also counted the small armada of
canoes at the fort. There were fifty made from birch
bark in the Indian style and over 170 pine dugouts.
George knew the canoes would be filled with French
soldiers and paddled down the Allegheny River into
the Ohio River in the spring. The French were planning to chase the British off "their" land. Indeed, St.
Pierre made it sound as though this would be no
more difficult than shaking the snow off his boots.

It was nearly Christmas, and the commander
insisted that George and his party accept two

canoes and a stash of food and fine wine to help them on their way back home. St. Pierre's behavior was confusing to George. No one at Fort le Boeuf appeared to view the Virginians as enemies. In fact, everyone had been courteous and made the Virginians' stay as enjoyable as possible. However, George learned that eight British traders had just been captured by the French and sent to France for trial, and another eight less fortunate ones had been scalped. Obviously the French did not consider George Washington and any information he could glean about them from his stay to be a threat. They were confident that the Ohio Valley would always belong to them.

George hoped for a fast trip back to Williamsburg to deliver Commander St. Pierre's reply and warn Governor Dinwiddie that the French planned a massive attack on British positions in the spring. However, since setting out from Williamsburg, a brutal winter had set in. For seven days the members of George's party took turns canoeing downstream and riding along the water's edge on exhausted horses. The churning water overturned the canoes, and one, along with many provisions, sank to the bottom. The party continued on with one canoe, which they sometimes had to lift out of the water and drag around obstacles.

By the time they reached Venango, where French Creek, which they had been following, emptied into the Allegheny River, George was becoming frustrated. The ice-packed river was slowing their progress, and he had promised to get the reply back to Governor Dinwiddie as soon as he could. George decided to set out on a more direct route on foot. He selected Christopher Gist, one of the Indian translators, to go with him while the rest of the men, along with the horses and remaining canoe, continued down the river at a slower pace.

The first day of their journey, George and Christopher trudged eighteen miles through knee-deep snow. As darkness descended that night, they reached a cabin, where a friendly Indian invited them to spend the night.

The following day they continued east, this time meeting up with another Indian, who offered to be their guide. At the time George thought this encounter was a stroke of luck because almost all the Indians in the Ohio Basin, except the Iroquois, were pro-French and anti-English. He soon discovered this particular Indian was not as friendly as he pretended to be.

After several hours of walking, George's feet were blistered and cold, and his fingers were beginning to feel as though they were frostbitten. He knew he had to rest. "Tell the Indian we're stopping for a while," he told Christopher.

Christopher relayed the message, but the Indian did not stop. George watched as the Indian continued on about fifteen yards, turned, put his gun to his shoulder, and took aim at Christopher. Boom! A shot echoed through the snowy wilderness. The bullet missed its mark, and George watched as Christopher leapt at the Indian, who was fumbling to reload his rifle. George sprinted over to them. He and Christopher managed to wrestle the rifle from the Indian.

"I'm going to slit his throat," Christopher growled as he reached for his hunting knife.

"No, don't do that!" George said. "We'll find a way to get out of this without killing him."

The Indian lay in the snow, his eyes wild with fear.

"Tell him to head off that way," George said, inclining his head to the north. "And tell him that if we catch another glimpse of him, we'll put a bullet through his skull."

"We should do it now," Christopher grumbled, and then he translated George's message for the Indian, who did not appear to believe it at first. Eventually, though, the Indian stood up and bolted into the stand of oak trees.

"We can't stay here," George said. "He could come back and bring his friends with him. Let's keep moving."

And move they did. Even though George could feel blood seeping from his blistered feet into his boots, the men did not dare stop walking for twenty-four hours.

It took another whole day of walking before the two men reached the spot where they needed to cross the Allegheny River. George's heart sank when he saw the river. He'd hoped it would be frozen all the way across by now, but between the ice packs that had built up along each shore was a hundred-yard-wide raging torrent of ice-cold water, with large chunks of ice bobbing along on top. If Commander

St. Pierre's reply was to be delivered, the two men would have to find a way across the river. After discussing the problem for a few minutes, they decided their best chance was to build a raft and try to pole their way across. The next morning they set about cutting down several trees to form the raft. It was a slow process, as they had only one small hatchet between the two of them. By late afternoon, though, a makeshift raft was floating at the edge of the ice. George and Christopher loaded their gear and themselves onto the raft and began to pole themselves out into the Allegheny River.

It was precarious navigating the ferocious current, and the more so when large blocks of ice slammed into the raft, twisting it off course. One of these blocks of ice hit the raft just as George dug his pole in and pushed with all his might to move them across the current. The raft slammed into the pole, launching George overboard. The icy water that surged around George took his breath away. As he gasped for air, he reached out and managed to grasp the end of one of the logs that formed the raft. He held on tightly until another block of ice collided with the raft, this time swamping it and sending Christopher into the water. George reached for his partner, and together they kicked against the current and the cold as best they could. Finally they could feel river bottom beneath them. They dragged themselves ashore and collapsed. They were stranded on a small island in the river, and they spent the night there huddled together for warmth in their wet clothes.

By morning George's buckskin clothes had frozen solid, and frostbite had set in on Christopher's fingers. However, there was some good news. During the night the river between the island and the shore had frozen over, and the ice was thick enough for the two men to walk on. Finally, wet and bedraggled, they made it across the Allegheny River.

After warming up and drying their clothes, George and Christopher made their way to Frazier's trading post several miles away. There George purchased a horse and headed on horseback southward along the Monongahela River until turning east and traveling through the Cumberland Gap.

It was a grueling journey. On January 16 an exhausted George Washington arrived in Williamsburg. It had been eleven weeks since he had set out from Virginia on the mission.

Governor Dinwiddie was pleased and a little surprised to see George back so soon. After reading the letter from Commander St. Pierre stating that he had no intention of leaving "French" territory, the governor asked George to write a report about all that he had seen and heard while at Fort le Boeuf. Many people read the report, and soon George Washington and his daring journey were the talk of the town. George felt a little embarrassed at being thrust into the limelight. He had no idea that as a result of his next expedition his name would be mentioned in the headlines in newspapers in Europe.

Chapter 6

Fort Necessity

By March 20, 1754, two separate bands of soldiers were on their way to stop the French from establishing a fort on the Ohio River, and a third band was preparing to leave Virginia to join the other two. The first band consisted of forty woodsmen led by Captain William Trent. The men had been sent out to build a fort on the river. Not far behind them were 134 men under the command of newly promoted Colonel George Washington. This band had most of the supplies with them. Finally, Colonel Joshua Fry, an elderly mathematics professor whom Governor Dinwiddie had put in command of the whole operation, was awaiting the arrival of the fighting men promised by the other colonies before setting out.

The whole approach to this campaign, which had been orchestrated by Governor Dinwiddie, seemed backward. First, the governor had sent out a captain, followed by George Washington, who was second in command. And while they marched out to confront the French, the commander of the campaign was not yet sure when he would join his troops in the field! Indeed, Joshua Fry had never even been in a battle before, though he had read about many of them.

Despite the disorganization, George Washington was a man under orders, and he decided he would make the best decisions he could until Colonel Fry arrived on the scene. George had with him very specific orders regarding what to do when he encountered the French. He was instructed not to attack. However, the orders also said, "In case any attempts are made to obstruct the works or interrupt our settlements by any persons whatsoever you are to restrain all such offenders and in case of resistance to make prisoners of or kill and destroy them."

George set out with a dozen carts and wagons laden with food, tools, lead shot, rum, and gunpowder. He was hopeful that Captain Trent would have the fort finished by the time he and his men had slogged their way over the mountains, hacking out a path wide enough for the wagons as they went. The trail they cut was the first road to lead across the Allegheny Mountains into the Ohio Valley.

George and his men were not far from the Ohio River when they met up with Captain Trent and his woodsmen. George knew this meeting could only mean bad news. Captain Trent told George that about a thousand French soldiers had canoed down the river and surrounded his men as they built the British fort. The men feared for their lives, but the French officers just laughed at them and told them to run along back to Virginia where they belonged. As Captain Trent had led his men away, he had looked back to see the unfinished fort engulfed in flames. To make matters worse, Half-King, a Shawnee Indian leader, reported to Captain Trent that the French were building a massive fort of their own.

Twenty-two-year-old George Washington had no idea what to do. He could retreat to Virginia, but surely that would look like the act of a coward. He could stay put and wait for Colonel Fry, but he had no idea when he was going to arrive. Every day that he did nothing was another day for the French to strengthen their grip on the Ohio Valley. George also could take his men and any Indians he persuaded to join him and advance against the thousand French soldiers building their fort. But advance was a tricky word right at that moment. Governor Dinwiddie's instructions had been to only act in defense and not to provoke an attack. George reasoned, though, that the French had already started a conflict when they ousted Captain Trent's men and burned their fort. With that clear in his mind, George Washington looked for a way to attack the French.

On the afternoon of May 27 Half-King told George that he had spotted about thirty French soldiers camped under a rocky outcrop not too far away. This was the opportunity George was waiting for. Thirty French soldiers were beatable, while one thousand probably were not.

At ten that night, under the cover of darkness and in driving rain, George set out from his camp with forty of his fittest men and six Shawnee Indians. The men walked in single file, often losing their way and veering deep into the surrounding woods. It was nearly impossible for anyone to see the man in front of him through the driving rain. George counted heads every hour or so, and at about four o'clock in the morning he was not surprised to discover that the last seven of the men were missing.

It was sunrise when George called for the men to halt. According to Half-King they were nearly upon the group of French soldiers. George sent several of the Indians out to scout for them. A few minutes later they returned to tell George that the French camp was only half a mile up the trail.

George signaled for his men to move forward and surround the French. Each man crept silently into the forest. The men's lives depended on not being seen. Once they were in place, the men were not more than a hundred yards from their enemy. Most of the French soldiers were waking up, and a few were rolling up blankets and stuffing their packs.

"Fire!" George yelled as he pulled the trigger on his musket, which he had aimed at a French soldier who had just awakened.

As shots rang out, the French soldiers, their eyes wild with fear, grabbed their rifles. Fifteen minutes later it was all over. Ten French soldiers lay dead, and the other twenty-two had surrendered. Colonel Washington counted his own men. One man was missing and was later found shot to death.

"You shoot Ensign Jumonville!" yelled one of the French soldiers in broken English. "Papers! Papers!"

George looked over to see what the commotion was about. "Go and find out what that prisoner wants," he told one of his French-speaking men.

Several minutes later the soldier returned with a pile of blood-drenched papers and a grim look on his face.

"What is it?" George asked impatiently.

"The prisoner says they were on a mission to deliver these papers to us. They were not trying to kill us. Sir, I think we just killed an ambassador."

"Nonsense," George replied. "They'll say anything to get us to release them."

But as George found out soon enough, it was not nonsense at all. Ensign Jumonville was carrying a letter from the French government to the governor of Virginia. In his eagerness to attack, George Washington had managed to fire a shot that was heard around the world, a shot that started the Seven Years' War between England and France.

For now, though, George had other problems to be concerned about. What he should do next was first on the list. He hadn't thought things through very well, and now he and his men had killed nearly a dozen French soldiers and apparently an ambassador. And he had no orders to retreat until Colonel Fry arrived. There was only one thing to do: he and his men would have to build a fort and prepare to defend themselves.

Fort Necessity was not really big enough to warrant the title "fort." It was built quickly with eight-foot-high walls made of oak logs. After it was erected, George waited anxiously for the promised reinforcements to arrive. Ten days later the first few of these men came straggling in with bad news. Colonel Fry had been knocked off his horse in a skirmish with the Indians and killed. That meant that George Washington, as the highest ranking officer, was now in charge of the operation.

More troops arrived, and by the beginning of July, 293 soldiers were assembled in and around Fort Necessity. Because the fort was so small, the entire regiment could not all fit comfortably inside the barricade at one time. The men began digging trenches around the fort in preparation to defend their position against the French.

As dawn broke on July 3, 1754, a steady rain fell, making life miserable for the men at Fort Necessity. As quickly as the men dug new trenches, the trenches began to fill with mud. Still, the men kept digging—their lives depended on it. At eleven in the morning one of the sentries spotted the French marching out from the trees on the high ground to the west of the fort.

The French soldiers under the command of Coulon de Villiers took up positions and opened fire on Fort Necessity. Immediately George ordered his men to fall into formation and marched them out to confront the French. He hoped to surround the French troops and defeat them on the open ground where they had massed. However, de Villiers ordered his men to fall back among the trees, where they were well camouflaged—so well camouflaged that George's men couldn't see them. But the French soldiers could see George's men in the open and began firing at them relentlessly. Men began to fall dead all around, and George realized he had been outmaneuvered. He ordered his men to fall back to the fort.

At the fort the men took up positions in the muddy trenches, some standing waist-deep in water. As the rain continued to pour down, the men were forced to strip off their clothes to wrap around their rifles, trying to keep them and their gunpowder dry so that the weapons would fire properly. Men took up positions on the two swivel guns mounted on the wall of Fort Necessity.

The French continued to fire. Then, from among the trees, Indians allied with the French streamed out. As they charged the fort, the two large swivel guns opened fire. The Indians kept coming until so many of them had been killed that the remaining warriors retreated back into the trees.

In the meantime the French troops had fanned out and surrounded the fort on three sides. From their position among the trees, they fired at will, picking off George's men one by one.

Realizing they were surrounded, some of the men, without orders from George, retreated into

Fort Necessity. Their actions infuriated George, who was not a man to retreat. Retreating wasn't in his plan. He was going to meet the French straight on and beat them. He was not going to run for the cover of the stockade. Still, despite his orders to the contrary, all the men had soon fled into the relative safety of the fort, and George was forced to follow. Now the French were free to close in and use the trenches the men had dug to fire on Fort Necessity.

Inside the crowded fort the men took up positions and returned fire. On they went throughout the afternoon, being fired at and returning gunfire. As the French tightened their noose around the fort, they shot and killed the garrison's horses and cattle, the men's main source of food. They even shot the dogs. And the French marksmen had finally found their range. Now as the soldiers raised their heads above the stockade to shoot at the French, the marksmen shot many of them. The casualties inside the fort began to mount, and George could see that the situation was becoming desperate.

To make matters worse, the torrential rain had not let up one bit all day. The men were soaked to the skin, and worse, moisture began to seep into their gunpowder, causing their muskets to misfire.

As a soaking darkness settled over Fort Necessity, the men inside began to despair. They feared the French would overrun them in the night and that the Indian allies of the French would then scalp them. In an attempt to try to suppress their fears, a number of the men broke into the rum supply and proceeded to drink themselves into a stupor.

Realizing the situation was hopeless, George decided it was time to negotiate. He sent interpreter Jacob Van Braam and another man out under a flag of truce. The two men crossed the French lines and began negotiations for surrender with de Villiers.

Later that night Van Braam returned to Fort Necessity with a document written in French by de Villiers. The ink was smudged by the constant rain, but once inside the fort, Van Braam translated it for George. Basically the document called for an honorable surrender. It allowed George Washington and his men safe passage back to Virginia. In return George was to leave two of his officers behind as hostages until the safe return of the twenty-two French prisoners taken in the raid that killed the ambassador. These prisoners had already been sent on to Virginia and would have to be returned from there. And in signing the surrender document, George would also acknowledge France's claim to the Ohio region.

Sadly George signed the document. He had no option. If he did not sign, he and the men under his command would surely all be killed. Soon after he had signed his name and the men began their retreat from Fort Necessity, the torrential rain stopped. It was a bittersweet moment, and George dreaded the reception he would receive when he arrived back in Virginia.

Chapter 7

A Blood Bath

A week after the surrender, George and his men
met up with the long-awaited New York regiment, who had finally reached Winchester,
Virginia. How George wished they had arrived earlier. With the extra men and weapons he might not
have had to surrender Fort Necessity.

A letter from Governor Dinwiddie arrived at the
same time asking George to report to him in
Williamsburg. George set off on July 11, relieved to
take a break from leading his men. However, he
was in for a few surprises when he reached
Williamsburg. For one thing, the local people
hailed him as a hero! Even though George had surrendered to the French and lost a third of his men,
most people thought he had acted bravely, and
they blamed the New York regiment for showing up

too late to be of any use. George was even featured in an editorial in the *Virginia Gazette.* One man, though, was not impressed with George Washington and his handling of the situation. That man was Governor Dinwiddie, who considered the whole situation to be a fiasco and told George so to his face. He also told him that he was no longer a colonel in the Virginia militia. And not only did the governor demote George, he announced that he was sending for a professional army from England to come and do a proper job of ousting the French from the Ohio Valley. As far as Governor Dinwiddie was concerned, George could either go back to being captain or quit the militia.

George chose to quit the militia right there and then. He gathered up his belongings and rode back to Ferry Farm, determined to put his military career behind him and make a life for himself as a planter.

In the time George had been away, Sarah, his brother Lawrence's daughter, had died. This opened the way for George to rent Mount Vernon from his sister-in-law. And when she died, according to Lawrence's will, the plantation would become George's property.

The arrangements were made, and on December 17, 1754, George Washington threw a party to celebrate the signing of the lease for Mount Vernon, along with eighteen slaves. The next day he set to work rebuilding his dead brother's plantation. He enlarged the house and prepared the land for a new crop of tobacco. As he worked, George tried not to think too much about army life, because when he did, he recalled how much he loved the adventure and camaraderie of it all.

But in March 1755 neither George nor anyone else in the region could ignore the army. Sixteen ships sailed up the Potomac River to Alexandria. On board the ships were British Major General Edward Braddock and fifteen hundred British troops. Their mission was to march through northern Virginia, cross the Allegheny Mountains, and destroy Fort Duquesne, the French garrison at the head of the Ohio River. While the British were destroying the fort, two American regiments would be sent to clear the French out of their forts at Niagara and Lake Champlain.

The sight of hundreds of men clad in buff breeches and crisp red coats marching in lockstep to drums and fifes filled George with new thoughts about fighting and valor. Within a week he knew he had to be a part of General Braddock's army. But how? His pride made it impossible for him to accept the rank of captain. To make matters worse, the king had ordered a stop to colonials being given the rank of colonel. Still, George decided, there must be some way around the rules. There was. He wrote to General Braddock describing his military experience and offering to serve as an unpaid aide. That way he could learn a lot about military tactics without being assigned a rank.

General Braddock accepted George's offer. As soon as the tobacco crop was planted and his younger brother Jack had arrived to manage Mount

Vernon in his absence, George set out to rendezvous with General Braddock's army. On May 2, 1755, George arrived in Frederick, Maryland, where the British troops were now camped.

George found General Braddock hard at work trying to scrape together twenty-five hundred horses and two hundred wagons to haul food, supplies, and munitions over the Allegheny Mountains to the Ohio River. It proved to be a long and involved task, and the army did not get packed and on their way until the end of May. Even then, their progress was painfully slow, so much so that General Braddock began to be concerned that the French would have too much time to amass their troops to defend against the British onslaught. As a result, the general split his army into two groups. The first group, consisting of thirteen hundred of the best soldiers, including the 44th Irish regiment and four companies of Virginia light infantry, were sent on ahead. The rest, including the sick, were to follow up the rear with the heavy equipment. George accompanied General Braddock with the first group.

On July 8, 1755, the first group of soldiers reached the Monongahela River, just twelve miles from Fort Duquesne. That night the soldiers all went to sleep knowing that they would be up early to begin their assault on the French fort. Many of the men, including George, assumed the French would surrender early in the fight and send most of their troops north to defend Canada against the British. They could not have been more wrong.

When reveille sounded before dawn the next morning, George got up and dressed in his parade-ground uniform. He was still feeling weak from a bout of dysentery, but weak or not, there was no way he was going to miss out on the day's action.

George watched with pride as the first group of 350 men marched past in review. Their uniforms were spotless, and their polished muskets gleamed in the first light of dawn. More groups of men filed past in General Braddock's prearranged order.

Finally, at 9:30 A.M., George rode out with General Braddock to supervise the attack on Fort Duquesne. Because of his weakened state, George had three pillows strapped to his saddle to cushion him from the joggling of his horse. It embarrassed him to have to do this, but not so much as it would to stay behind at camp.

Things were going according to plan. At 2:30 in the afternoon one of the scouts reported to General Braddock that fifteen hundred soldiers were less than seven miles from the fort and that George and the general were a mile behind these men. A smile of satisfaction spread across General Braddock's face. "Perfect. Everything is going according to plan," he muttered.

The words had no sooner left his lips than the sound of gunfire reverberated from the woods ahead. It wasn't constant, just a few shots here and there. George halted his horse and turned to face General Braddock. What could it be? The British were not yet close enough to have opened fire on the French. Suddenly the sound of a constant volley of gunfire filled the air, and then it settled back into the pattern of intermittent shots.

"Forward into battle," General Braddock yelled as he urged his horse forward. The men marching alongside surged through the path cut in the trees until they came upon the advance party of soldiers running wildly toward them.

"Where are your commanders?" General Braddock bellowed.

"Shot by Indians," a soldier with a wide gash across his forehead said frantically. "It's a blood bath."

George was stunned. He watched as the soldiers fleeing down the road collided with the men the general was leading. In the confusion the two groups bunched together, twelve abreast on the road. Also in the confusion George watched as the shadowy figures of Indians darted between the trees. As they did so, gunfire rained down on the British from among bushes, from behind trees, and from between gaps in the rocks. Several Indians ran out and dragged two dead soldiers into the woods. Minutes later the soldiers were thrown back into the confusion, minus their scalps!

Panic followed as men clawed over one another to try to get out of reach of the Indians. Gunsmoke stung George's eyes, making it nearly impossible for him to get a clear view of all that was going on.

"They're behind us!" came a yell. Pandemonium broke out as all the men bolted back down the road. Many dropped their guns and began a desperate sprint for the river.

George sprang into action, urging his horse on among the terrified men. "Don't retreat!" he shouted. "Stop and turn around."

But the men had no intention of turning around. George looked over to see General Braddock flailing the flat side of his sword at the men who dared to hide among the bushes. "Into formation!" he was yelling at the top of his lungs.

George turned his horse and galloped over to the general. "Sir," he screamed, "let the men scatter into the trees. At least we have a chance that way."

"No," the general responded, "that's not the British way. They must stand tall and fight like men."

George's heart sank. Unless they changed their tactics fast, the bloodshed would continue. Their only hope was to fight the Indians the Indian way—scattered among the trees.

General Braddock kept yelling and slashing at any soldiers who dared to hide from the battle.

By now French soldiers had reinforced the Indians, and together they continued to pick off the redcoats one at a time. The officers, who were on horseback, were easy targets. George watched as a bullet tore through General Braddock's arm and into his chest. He had to reach the general. At that moment George's horse was shot through the head and toppled to the ground. George dragged himself out from under the dead animal's massive body and grabbed the reins of a riderless horse. He leapt into the saddle and galloped in the direction where General Braddock had fallen.

"Go for reinforcements," the general gasped at George.

George took one last look at the piles of bodies heaped up on the road. "Yes, sir," he replied as he turned and galloped off.

Soon the sound of the battle faded from hearing, but George knew that if he lived to be one hundred years old, the horrid sight he had just witnessed would never fade from his memory. He rode on alone into the night until he reached the place forty miles away where the reinforcements were encamped. After delivering General Braddock's order for reinforcements, George fell onto a camp bed utterly exhausted. As he took off his coat, he was amazed to count four bullet holes through it, and one more in his hat. Waves of nausea washed over him as he went to sleep thinking about the savagery he had witnessed that day.

It was well into the following day before George awoke to the bad news. There was no hope for the British. They had been outmaneuvered. George rode back to the frontline, where he found General Braddock dying. What was left of the British army fled to Philadelphia, while George, weary and homesick, retreated to Mount Vernon.

It wasn't long before the numbers of dead and wounded from the battle were tallied. Every Virginia officer except for George Washington had been killed or wounded, as were sixty-three of the eighty-six British officers. Among the enlisted men, the numbers were just as grim. Out of the 1,373 enlisted men who took part in the battle, 914 were dead or wounded. And many of the wounded were lying in makeshift hospital barracks enduring slow and painful deaths.

The immensity of all that had happened weighed on George's mind as he rode onto his plantation. He was sure General Braddock's defeat would reflect poorly on all of the officers. However, George was surprised to find that his colonial Virginia neighbors welcomed him as a hero once again. News of his bravery in battle had gone before him, and people would not let George settle back into plantation life. There was too much to do. Not only had the British been routed by the French, they had also abandoned Fort Cumberland, leaving western Virginia defenseless. Horrific stories of bands of up to 150 Shawnee Indians attacking Virginians on remote farms struck terror into the hearts of everyone who heard them. Within weeks of George's return, over seventy settlers had been murdered and their farm buildings razed.

A public outcry went forth. Something had to be done to make the western borders safe from attack. Governor Dinwiddie knew of only one man who could restore the confidence of his colony— George Washington. So in spite of the king's ban on promoting colonials to the rank of colonel, within weeks of his return to Mount Vernon George was given the position of colonel of the Virginia regiment and commander in chief of all Virginia forces. At twenty-three years of age, he was the highest-ranked military man in the colonies.

For the next three years George Washington commanded an army that defended Virginia's western border from French and Indian attack. It was a difficult task, made nearly impossible by the shortage of money and good men for the militia and the constantly changing expectations of the British in their fight with the French.

Throughout this time illness plagued George, as it did most of those under his command. The standard treatment for fever at the time was to be bled, a practice whereby a doctor cut into a vein and let blood flow out in the mistaken belief that the blood would take with it the sickness or fever. However, the practice only served to weaken a patient further, as was the case with George. By November 1, 1757, George was so weak from dysentery that he could hardly walk. He had been bled three times in two days, and when the procedure only made him weaker, Dr. Craik urged him to return to Mount Vernon for a long rest. Otherwise, the doctor warned, George would die. It was enough warning for George, who set out immediately for home, where he climbed into a comfortable bed and enjoyed hot, nutritious meals.

As George began to recover from the violent cramping effects of dysentery, another ailment took over, a hacking cough and sore lungs. George lay in the same bed in which his brother Lawrence had died, thinking morbid thoughts. Surely, he told himself, he had tuberculosis and would die the same way Lawrence had. Weeks went by, and George got worse. Finally, he could not stand thinking about the possibility of his own death anymore. He was determined to get to a doctor who could tell him whether he really did have tuberculosis or something less ominous.

With a great deal of help, George managed to ride to Williamsburg in early April 1758. He made an appointment with Dr. Amson, one of the leading doctors in the colony, and received good news. He was suffering not from tuberculosis but from a nagging cough caused by fatigue and a long, cold winter. Just hearing the news made George feel better, and within a few days he was cheerful and optimistic again. He wasn't going to die after all!

In fact, George Washington was feeling so much happier that he decided to stop in and see an acquaintance, Major William Chamberlayne, on the way home. William Chamberlayne's plantation was located about thirty miles northwest of Williamsburg on the banks of the tidal Pamunkey River, a tributary of the York. It was during this visit that George had a chance meeting with William's next-door neighbor. It was a meeting that would bring great change to George Washington's life.

Chapter 8

A Quietly Capable Woman

George climbed the steps of William Chamberlayne's plantation house. He was looking forward to catching up on the latest news of the war with France from the major. From what he had heard in Williamsburg, the tide had turned and the British were beginning to get the upper hand.

William greeted George warmly at the door, and before long the two men were sitting in the major's library beside a roaring fire.

"So what do you make of William Pitt?" George quizzed his host. William Pitt was the new leader of Parliament in England.

Major Chamberlayne smiled. "Thank goodness we finally have someone who is prepared to do something! I just reviewed several documents outlining some new strategies for the fighting this morning. I am sure the same documents will be waiting for you to review when you get back to Mount Vernon."

"What do they say?" George asked.

"Great news, really; no more dallying about. Young Pitt is getting much more aggressive in the Atlantic, and the French are having a hard job getting a single ship with troops and supplies through to Canada. They'll never keep the Indians loyal to them unless they keep bribing them with goods." William leaned back and took a drink of brandy. "I predict the war will be over by the end of the year," he then added.

"You think the fighting at sea will be enough to bring France to its knees?" George asked.

"Oh no! Pitt has other plans too. He's a man of action. The papers outline three land attacks to be launched against the French all at the same time."

George leaned forward, his eyebrows raised. He had been hoping for months now to hear about the possibility of some real action.

"We're going to hit the French at Fort Duquesne, at Ticonderoga in northern New York, and at Louisburg."

"Louisburg! I see what you mean. That's a bold move, attacking them inside Canada. Let's hope we make short work of them. The colonists' patience is beginning to run out."

William nodded. "Yes, it's gone on for much longer than anyone would have predicted. I assume

Pitt will put you and your soldiers under General Forbes's command because..."

A knock at the door interrupted the conversation. A slave scurried to the door and let in a short woman wearing a black dress.

Major Chamberlayne jumped to his feet. "Come in, my dear," he said.

The woman stopped when she saw George getting to his feet. "Oh, I am so sorry to interrupt your meeting. I had no idea you had a guest. I was just returning a book, but I can do it another time." She began to back out of the room.

"No, no. Please stay, Mrs. Custis," William said. "You are not an interruption at all. I take it you are acquainted with Colonel Washington."

George bowed. "I am delighted to meet you again, Mrs. Custis," George said. "And I am very sorry to hear of your recent loss."

Martha Dandridge Custis smiled shyly. "Thank you. It is an honor to meet you again. You must know you have made quite a name for yourself in Virginia. We are all counting on you to win the war for us."

George felt himself turning red. He seldom found himself in the company of a woman. "Please, take a seat," he stammered, offering her the spot by the fire where he had been sitting.

As Martha walked past George, he looked down at her, and down it was. She was only four feet ten inches tall, over a foot shorter than he was. Of course George had seen Martha before at social functions, but she had been a married woman then. Now she was a twenty-five-year-old widow to whom George found himself drawn. There was something calm and peaceful about Martha.

William invited Martha to join them for dinner, and that night, as they ate, George found himself less interested in talking about the war and more interested in learning about Martha. He learned that she had two children, Jacky (John), who was three years old, and Patsy (Martha), who was eighteen months old. Indeed, the children were eating upstairs with their nanny. George also discovered that Martha liked visiting the Chamberlayne home in an effort to get some privacy. In the months since her husband, Daniel, had died, she had been subjected to a steady stream of visitors, many of them men who said they were coming to pay their respects to her dead husband. However, Martha decided many of them were more interested in getting their hands on her money. After all, she was the richest widow in all Virginia.

"Would you like to meet my children?" Martha asked as lemon tart was being served for dessert.

"Very much," George replied. He had a soft spot for children. By now he had nine nieces and nephews of his own.

By the end of the evening George knew he wanted to spend more time with this woman who was quietly capable of running her own plantation. The following morning before he left, George accepted an invitation to visit Martha in her own home, which she called the "White House."

Within a week George was back with plans to ask Martha Custis to be his wife. He wasn't sure if he was in love, but he felt his affection for her would grow over time. Martha possessed many of the qualities he wanted in a wife, and he already liked Jacky and Patsy. George was confident he would be a good stepfather to them. After a short twenty-four hours together, George asked for Martha's hand in marriage. Much to his relief, she immediately agreed, though they did not set a wedding date. Now that George was feeling better, it was time for him to resume command of the Virginia regiment. But as he and Martha talked about their future together, George discovered that what he wanted more than anything else was to live the quiet life of a plantation owner. A life set by the rhythm of the seasons, of planting, growing, and harvesting the tobacco crop, with a wife at his side and a handful of children running around.

Excitement about the future coursed through George as he journeyed back to take command of the militia. Now that the war was turning in Britain's favor, George hoped to be discharged from the military as soon as was practical. With this in mind, he applied to run for a seat in the House of Burgesses from Frederick County. The House of Burgesses was Virginia's representative assembly, of which his brother Lawrence had been a member before his death. Although George Washington was too far away to campaign for the position, George Fairfax stirred up interest in him as a delegate.

George Washington won over the sitting member by a wide margin.

Thursday, November 24, 1758, was the day Colonel George Washington had been looking forward to for a long time. It was the day the French military, realizing that its supply line from France had been cut, burned Fort Duquesne to the ground and fled up the Allegheny River. Now, at last, the English had control of the Ohio Valley.

There were still many battles to fight, but as far as George was concerned, they were not his battles. He had completed his mission to secure Virginia's borders from the French and Indians. Now he felt free to resign and begin his new life.

George was discharged from the military and returned to Mount Vernon in time for Christmas. In the time since he had proposed to Martha, George had ordered some major changes to his home. In George's absence a master builder had expanded the one-and-one-half-story farmhouse, raising the roof and making the house into a full two-story house with four rooms upstairs and four rooms downstairs. George was especially pleased with the new stairway, modeled after the latest fashion in elegant English homes.

On the day after Christmas 1758 George Washington, accompanied by Sally and George Fairfax, set out for the home of Martha Custis. After their two-day carriage ride in freezing weather, Martha welcomed the three weary travelers into her home. She was efficient and kind and just as George remembered her from when he had proposed. Patsy was shy at first, but Jacky climbed onto George's knee and played with the buttons on his vest.

There were ten days until the wedding, and George had a lot to do. Since Daniel Custis had died without leaving a will, all of his land, slaves, and money were divided equally among Martha, Patsy, and Jacky. However, in Virginia it was illegal for a married woman to have any property in her own name. Everything she owned before a wedding had to be given to her new husband. So George prepared the papers to transfer ownership of all Martha's assets to him. It was a complicated process, made more difficult because when he married Martha, George would also become responsible for the children's share of the estate until they came of age.

The time passed quickly, and the White House began to fill with guests from neighboring plantations, including some of Martha's brothers and sisters. The new royal governor of Virginia, Francis Fauquier, arrived on the bitter cold afternoon before the wedding. He was just in time for a lively evening of country dancing. Everyone went to bed exhausted in the early hours of the morning. That day, January 6, 1759, George Washington and Martha Custis were married in Martha's living room. The service was followed by two more days and nights of feasts, dancing, and endless rounds of toasts to the new couple. Finally, three days after the wedding, the guests departed, leaving the new Mr. and Mrs. Washington to get to know each other better.

The newlyweds stayed at the White House until mid-February, when it was time for George to take his place as a member of the Virginia House of Burgesses in Williamsburg. He looked forward to seeing George Fairfax again, but he was a little nervous about his new job. He realized he knew more than most men about war but not much about politics. The subject had never really interested him, though he would not admit it to those around him. More than any other reason, George had become a member of the Houses of Burgesses to keep a watch over new laws that were likely to affect his land holdings. He decided to keep his mouth shut and his eyes open unless the discussion concerned something he knew a lot about.

By April the session of the House of Burgesses was over, and George began planning the 160-mile trip from Williamsburg to Mount Vernon via the White House. It reminded him of planning a military operation. Naturally enough, Martha wanted to take many belongings from her old home with her, and she had thousands of items and many slaves to transport. The list grew daily, until George had to figure a way to get ten beds, piles of feather quilts and blankets, desks, mirrors, a large mahogany dining table, and trunks filled with tablecloths and napkins, silver, china, pots, ladles, buckets, fabric, coffee mills, and wine glasses to Mount Vernon. The enormous task was made all the more difficult because George was responsible for making sure that everything was meticulously recorded in a 247-column ledger. After all, two-thirds of everything belonged to Patsy and Jacky, and George was required to submit a written statement twice a year regarding the whereabouts and condition of their belongings to the general court of Virginia.

George and Martha arrived at Mount Vernon just in time to supervise the transplanting of the young tobacco plants into rows three feet apart. Martha's field slaves would be useful in the continuous hoeing of weeds that would start a week later.

Life at the plantation was quite different now that George had a wife and two stepchildren. Martha proved to be a wonderful cook and hostess, and soon a steady stream of visitors came knocking at the door. Some of them were good friends of George from his army days. Others were strangers, friends of friends who needed a place to stay for the night. No matter who they were, George and Martha made them welcome.

George had hoped the years after his marriage would be punctuated by the births of several children, but he and Martha remained childless. Instead it was the price George got for his tobacco crops that made one year different from the next.

The first year he was married, George made a good profit on the tobacco that he sent to England for sale. The following year, 1760, though, was not so good. It rained more than usual that year, ruining much of the crop, and the tobacco that was sent sold for a very low price in England. It was a disaster for George and for many of the other Virginia planters. Tobacco was the only crop most of them grew. After the crop was dried, it was packed into one-thousand-pound hogshead barrels for shipment to England. If the shipment survived the voyage across the Atlantic Ocean, the tobacco was unloaded in England by an agent and sold. Planters in Virginia and the other colonies would also send a list of goods they wanted the agent to buy with the money from the sale. However, this led to big problems. When the planter sent the list, he had no idea how much money the tobacco would fetch at market or how much the goods he ordered would cost. And the situation was made worse by the fact that most agents found ways to cheat the colonists out of some of their money.

In 1760 George received the goods he ordered from England—and a sobering shock. The agent had spent nineteen hundred pounds more on the goods than he said he had been paid for George's tobacco. Indeed, George worked out that by the time all of the taxes, shipping insurance, and agent's fees had been paid, he was left with only a quarter of the money from the sale before the agent started purchasing goods for him!

This new debt made George furious. Radical thoughts flooded his mind. What if he forgot about sending goods to England altogether and concentrated on producing items that he could sell directly to other people in the colonies? George collected every book he could on how to grow things, and soon he set about experimenting with other crops and products. In 1761 Lawrence Washington's widow, Anne, died, and ownership of Mount

Vernon was transferred to George, who was determined to make a showcase of the plantation.

It was slow going, but in 1762 oats were
planted in some of Mount Vernon's fields. Just as
the crop was budding, George received the sad
news that his half brother, Austin, had died after a
long illness. Austin was forty-two years old and left
behind a wife and five children. George rode to
Westmoreland for the funeral. Now both of his
older brothers were dead, and George felt very vul-
nerable. He wondered if he would be the next to
die.

George continued experimenting with new
ideas, and under his steady hand, Mount Vernon
began to prosper. George also bought neighboring
land to add to the plantation and slaves to work
the soil. And while he was happy being a plantation owner, George also continued as a member of
the House of Burgesses and was elected church-
warden of Truro Parish. In February 1763 the
French and English signed the Treaty of Paris, officially ending the war between the two countries.
France had been soundly beaten in North America,
and England's new king, George III, had great
plans for Canada.

Unfortunately Britain was deeply in debt from
the Seven Years' War with France, and with King
George III's big ideas, new money had to come from
somewhere. For a start, the king felt it was only
fair for the colonies to pay for the British troops
who remained on the American continent to keep
various Indian tribes at bay. No one knew it then,

but the idea that the colonies should be taxed by Parliament to pay for things colonists had not voted for was a spark that would ignite into a great struggle with England and the king.

This spark started with something called the Stamp Act, which became law in 1765. This act decreed that every legal document transacted in the colonies had to have a blue paper seal on it called a stamp. And each stamp cost four shillings, as much as George Washington paid his farm managers for a week's work. The "tax" money raised from these stamps was to go directly back to England, where Parliament could spend it in whatever way it saw fit.

No one in the colonies was happy about the Stamp Act. The unified cry from people in the North American colonies was "No taxation without representation." Simply, this meant that unless they had their own representatives who could vote on taxes in the British Parliament, they would not accept being taxed. George and other plantation owners decided not to put anything aboard ships to England, since they would need papers that required stamps to do so. Instead the planters began to do what George had been moving toward for several years: they began growing crops that could be sold in the colonies. George was enthusiastic about this endeavor. He had a schooner built so that his servants and slaves could fish in the Potomac River. Flax was grown on the plantation and turned into linen thread that was woven into cloth, and a distillery was built, along with a flour mill. George even had a sawmill set up. Slowly Mount Vernon was being enlarged and transformed from a plantation to a small village.

A few plantation owners were tempted to pay the stamp tax and send their tobacco off to England anyway. But a group calling themselves the Sons of Liberty set about putting pressure on anyone who wanted to cave in and pay the tax.

By 1766 the British Parliament had gotten the message, and the Stamp Act was repealed. The colonists, including George Washington, felt they had made their point and that things would run smoothly between England and the colonies in the future. It would have been wonderful if that were the case, but the British Parliament had in fact replaced the Stamp Act with something far more sinister. This new law was called the Declaratory Act, and it stated that the king and Parliament "had, hath and of right ought to have the full power and authority to make laws and statues of suffi-cient force and validity to bind the Colonies and people of America, subjects of the Crown of Great Britain, in all cases whatsoever." In other words, Parliament may have agreed to remove the stamp tax, but in return it had voted itself the right to tax the American colonies in any way it chose in the future. Any colonist who refused to pay one of those taxes could be tried for treason and hanged.

Despite this new law most people in the colonies of North America were glad that the Stamp Act had been repealed. No one, including George, dreamed more conflict with the British lay ahead.

Chapter 9

A Growing Crisis

With the Stamp Act issue "solved," George Washington was free to put his efforts into buying more land, planting apple trees at Mount Vernon, and educating his two stepchildren. This proved to be a nearly impossible task in the case of Jacky, who had turned out to be everything George did not like—a young man who knew one day he would inherit a fortune and could not be bothered learning anything useful in the meantime.

To make matters worse, Martha doted on Jacky and made endless excuses for his rude, sulky behavior. By 1768 the fourteen-year-old needed a sterner hand than part-time tutors could provide, and George insisted that the boy be sent to boarding school in Annapolis, Maryland. Jacky wrote home to say he was not happy in his new situation, but George made him stay anyway. It was much more peaceful at Mount Vernon with Patsy as the only child in the house. She had a much different character than her brother. She was warm and funny, and George came to love her as his own daughter. Indeed, his favorite time of day was after dinner when Patsy would play her spinet for George and any guests who were in the house.

It was quite a shock, then, when on the night of June 13, 1768, George and Martha returned from a party at the Fairfaxes and found several servants standing over Patsy as she writhed on the floor in some kind of fit. George carried her to a couch and ordered a servant to fetch Dr. Rumney immediately. All at once Patsy went completely limp. George felt her wrist. Her heart was still beating. By the time the doctor arrived, Patsy was sitting up, but he bled her anyway and gave her drops for her '"nerves." Dr. Rumney told George and Martha this could be an isolated fit, or it could be the beginning of a serious problem for their daughter. Only time would tell.

Patsy continued to have fits, sometimes up to two a day. George tried every bit of medical advice he could find. He fed Patsy mercury pills and had "cramp" rings made for her fingers, hoping that these metal bands would ward off the fits. There were also trips to hot springs and the best doctors in Virginia, but nothing helped. The Washingtons realized that all they could do was to make Patsy's life as happy and normal as they could and hope that in time she would grow out of her condition.

By early 1769, for the first time in his life, George Washington's attention was firmly fixed on political matters. The British Parliament, under the advice of Lord Townshend, had imposed a whole new level of taxes on the American colonies. These were much harsher than the Stamp Act and included a tax on glass, lead, paper, and tea. To justify its action, Parliament cited the Declaratory Act. This enraged George, who with another member of the House of Burgesses, George Mason, decided it was time for Virginia to act. The people of the colony should band together and establish a "nonimportation" agreement, by which people promised to buy virtually nothing from England or her other colonies around the world.

A meeting of the House of Burgesses began on May 8, 1769, and several new members were in attendance, including a young lawyer named Thomas Jefferson, representing Albemarle County, and Patrick Henry from Hanover County. However, the meeting did not follow its routine for long. When Virginia's governor heard of the plan by the House of Burgesses to call for a boycott on imported goods, he became furious. He immediately ordered the House of Burgesses dissolved and told everyone, including George Washington, to return home.

The members of the House of Burgesses were appalled. The House of Burgesses had been meeting for 150 years to make laws regarding issues involving their colony. Now, with the wave of his hand, the governor expected them all to give up and go home! They would not. Instead, they marched en masse down Duke of Gloucester Street and crowded into Raleigh Tavern, where they continued their discussions. The following morning George was appointed the chairman of a committee to look into an embargo on British goods.

On September 1 George presented the committee's recommendations to what had been the House of Burgesses. The report recommended that the import of numerous goods, including slaves, wine, cheese, oil, furniture, fabric, clocks, mirrors, boots, and jewelry, be banned. A vote was taken, with ninety-four votes for the embargo and twenty-two against it. George had gotten his way. The beer and wine flowed as the ex-burgesses celebrated a decision that would soon make each of their lives more difficult as the flow of goods into Virginia was curtailed.

George read about how other colonies were standing up for their rights. In March 1770, for instance, Boston grew tired of having to host the thousands of British troops who were stationed there. A riot broke out in front of the Customs House, and the redcoats fired on the colonists. When the smoke had cleared, five Bostonians were dead and seven more were wounded. The shooting was labeled "The Boston Massacre," and Paul Revere's etching of the incident was circulated to all thirteen colonies. When George saw the etching and read the story, he was troubled. The British troops seemed a little too eager to fire on the colonists. Would they be even more eager to shoot the next time there was a disagreement?

The next three years were tense for everyone. George watched as the British government tried to force the America colonies to do certain things and then quietly backed away from them when the colonists stood their ground. Eventually the Townshend taxes, except for the tax on tea, were withdrawn, and the colonies went back to ordering goods from the mother country.

George was happy with the results of the boycott. He felt confident that the colonies had sent Britain a serious message and that Parliament and King George would be more cautious next time they thought about taxing colonists. But there was still the matter of the tea tax. George thought it was nothing to be concerned about. After all, it was only three pennies a pound, nothing compared to all the other taxes the Townshend Act had levied on them. But not everyone agreed with George's view, especially the citizens of Boston, where anti-British feelings still ran high.

While all this pushing and pulling between England and the colonies was going on, Patsy continued to suffer from fits. On July 19, 1773, a large group sat down to dinner at Mount Vernon. Among the guests were George's brother Jack and his family, Jacky Custis's fiancée, sixteen-year-old Nelly (Eleanor) Calvert, and a friend of Nelly's. The soup course was just being served when Patsy fell from her chair. George lunged to help her, but there was nothing he or anyone else could do. Patsy lay still and lifeless on the wooden floor. George, barely aware of Martha's screaming, sat staring at his stepdaughter as the color drained from her face.

Patsy's funeral was a sober affair, made more so by the news that George's oldest friends George and Sally Fairfax were traveling to England and would not be returning for a long time, if ever. There were two reasons for their trip: Sally Fairfax was ill, and George Fairfax was loyal to the British Crown and feared the brewing crisis in the colonies.

The months that followed Patsy's death were among the loneliest George had ever faced. He tried to comfort his wife, but there were no words that could help her with her grief. To make matters worse, Jacky, who was only eighteen years old, was pushing for an early wedding. Neither George nor Martha thought Jacky was mature enough to marry, and they had insisted that if the young couple did get engaged, they were not to marry for several years. Now, much to George's annoyance, Jacky was taking advantage of his mother's weakened state to call for a wedding.

In the end the Washingtons gave in, and a wedding was set for February 1774. Just over a month before the wedding was due to take place, yet another flare-up occurred between Britain and an American colony. It happened as a result of the Tea Act, by which Parliament in England gave the British East India Company the right to be the only merchants who were allowed to import tea into the American colonies. Soon people in Massachusetts were asking a big question: What if this was only the beginning and slowly Britain gave away the rights to import all sorts of things into the colonies? American importers would be driven out of business, and colonists would have to pay whatever prices the monopolies asked for their goods.

Tempers ran high in Boston on December 23, 1773. A group of 150 merchants, lawyers, and artisans dressed as Mohawk Indians rushed down to the docks and boarded the East India Company ship *Dartmouth*, which carried the first shipment of tea to the colony under the Tea Act. The men pulled 342 boxes of tea up onto the deck, smashed them open with tomahawks, and dumped the tea into Boston Harbor.

It took over a week for news of the Boston Tea Party to reach Mount Vernon. As George listened to the messenger, he worried about what would happen next. It did not seem to him a wise move to stir up the British, especially when the tea the "Indians" had dumped into the harbor was worth over ten thousand pounds. Surely, he told Martha later that evening, the British would make someone pay for it one way or another.

As planned, Jacky and Nelly Custis were married in February 1774 at the bride's home in Maryland. George went alone to the ceremony. He could not coax Martha to take the long carriage trip. Martha did, however, let George talk her into accompanying him as far as Williamsburg. As they stopped at homes along the way, it seemed to George as if the entire countryside was in an uproar. It all had to do with the newly announced punishment Britain was forcing on Boston for throwing all of that tea into the harbor. The Boston Port Bill, as it was called, forbade any loading or unloading of ships in Boston, which was New England's main port. Most of the citizens of Boston relied on shipping in one way or another, and thousands of people were instantly out of jobs. Parliament announced that the harbor would not be opened again until someone in Boston paid for all the tea that had been poured into the harbor. A second bill passed by Parliament authorized the governor of Massachusetts to send political prisoners or those who took part in riots back to England for trial. These people were not to be tried in the colony, as in the past.

Normally, a law passed by Parliament regarding one colony was largely ignored by people in the other colonies. After all, each colony had its own special arrangements with Britain. But this time something different happened. People from New Hampshire to Georgia began to think of themselves as a single group, one people living on the edge of a vast continent.

This change in thinking was reflected in a vote that George Washington and the other members of the Virginia House of Burgesses took. Following a stirring speech from Thomas Jefferson, George voted to make June 1, 1774, the day when Boston Harbor would officially be shut down, a day of fasting and prayer for all of the colonies. This action angered the governor of Virginia, Lord Dunmore, who especially disliked the words, "We are further clearly of opinion, that an attack, made on one of our sister Colonies, to compel submission to arbitrary taxes, is an attack made on all British America, and threatens ruin to the rights of all." Lord Dunmore was amazed and shocked to see the phrase "sister colonies" used. The words suggested that the colonies were aligning with one another rather than each looking individually to Britain for its guidance. Once again the governor dissolved the Virginia House of Burgesses. And once again George and the other men marched down Duke of Gloucester Street to reconvene their meeting at Raleigh Tavern.

Some of the same old discussions and resolutions were passed at the meeting. The "ex-burgesses" voted for an embargo on all imported goods from England, but this time they did something they had not done before, something for which each of them could hang for treason. The hundred or so men listened as Thomas Jefferson explained "that we must boldly take an unequivocal stand in the line with Massachusetts," because when Britain attacked one colony it was really attacking all of them as *Americans*. This was a new and revolutionary thing to say, but something about what Jefferson said resonated deeply within George Washington. It was time for the colonies to stand up for one another and join together as one force against England. The men made a resolution calling for each colony to send representatives to a convention that would have one objective in mind: to explore the possibility of a new government made up of colonists who would make all of their own laws.

George Washington was the eighth person to cast his vote in favor of the convention. He knew it was treason, but he did not care. Something had to be done about the British and their unfair laws.

On June 1, 1774, George and Martha Washington fasted and spent the day at church praying for whatever lay ahead for them and the colonies. George prayed especially hard, since he had been elected along with five other delegates, including Peyton Randolph, Richard Henry Lee, and Patrick Henry, to represent Virginia at the gathering of representatives from the colonies. The meeting was scheduled to be held in Philadelphia in September. Philadelphia had been chosen because it was midway between New England and the southern colonies.

George had a lot to do before September. For one thing he was in the middle of adding a new wing to Mount Vernon. This addition was partly to take Martha's mind off Patsy's death and partly because they needed the room for the visitors who came to their door. The alterations included a new ninety-foot-long veranda so that in the evening the Washingtons and their guests could sit in rocking chairs and watch the Potomac flow by. A new library, master bedroom, and ballroom were all part of the new structure, which was joined to the original house by a long covered walkway.

A hot southerly wind blew on August 30 as George Washington made final plans to travel to

Philadelphia. That night George, Patrick Henry, and several of the other delegates gathered at Mount Vernon. They spent the evening discussing what might happen at the Continental Congress, as the meeting was now being called. No one knew for sure what lay ahead. Would all of the colonies send representatives? Was it likely, or even possible, that so many representatives from such different colonies could agree on what step to take next? And if they didn't, should those colonies that could agree band together and leave the others out? These were questions that were impossible for George to answer, and just as impossible for him to put out of his mind. He would just have to wait and see.

Chapter 10

General George Washington

George Washington and the other Virginia delegates reached Philadelphia on September 4,
1774. There they stayed at the stately home of one
of the delegates' sister. The next morning over seventy men, representing every colony except
Georgia, gathered in the city tavern and got down
to business.

The delegates from other colonies fascinated
George. The majority of them came from other royal
colonies, like Virginia, where the king appointed
the governor. But some of the delegates were from
the so-called proprietary colonies of Pennsylvania,
Delaware, and Maryland, where the governor was
appointed by the proprietor of the colony. And
there were delegates from the two self-governing
colonies of Rhode Island and Connecticut, whose

governors were elected by voters. Yet no matter how the governor of each colony was chosen, all the colonies had one thing in common: they all had a written charter from the King of England granting them certain rights and privileges. But now they felt the king was not honoring those rights and privileges, and they had gathered to see what could be done about it.

It did not take the men long to make the initial two decisions. First they elected Peyton Randolph to be president of the First Continental Congress; then they accepted the offer of the carpenters' union to use its hall as a meeting place. Many of the delegates, including George, soon wondered whether this had been a good choice. Once it got under way, the Congress met six days a week for the duration. Since the meetings were secret, all of the windows were kept shut and the doors locked. The hall was soon filled with the smell of sweat and thousands of flies. It was not the sort of place George or many of the other rich leaders were used to meeting in, but the men returned day after day to hammer out some kind of agreement on what they should do next.

It took six weeks, but finally they all agreed to two major actions. The first was the Declaration of Rights, which explained how, in the colonists' opinion, Parliament had violated their rights. The second was a ban on imported goods from England. Rather than just leave it up to individual citizens to refrain from buying goods from England, the Congress set up the Continental Association, an agreement by all the colonies to stick to the boycott. To make sure this was the case, each colony present promised to create local committees who would make sure that no one in their village or county broke the boycott. The punishment for such a breach was the public disgrace of being tarred and feathered.

George wanted to push the issue further. He wanted a ban on all exports from the colonies as well, but many of the other delegates thought this was too harsh. In the end it was decided that exports should last another year so that plantation owners could get one more crop to market before cutting themselves off from their source of income.

Some of the delegates were all for fighting England to get their rights, while others hoped that writing a strongly worded letter to King George III followed by the boycott would get their message across. The Continental Congress decided that it would plan another meeting in seven months' time, but only if relations with England had not improved.

As George began the ride back to Virginia, he was hopeful the situation would improve, but in the six weeks he had been away the mood in Virginia had turned ugly. Many men had banded together to form militias, some wanting to defend their property and others to strike out at British targets. George was alarmed at this turn of events. Writing letters to the king and boycotting goods was one thing, but war with the most powerful empire on earth was quite another!

Indeed, George was still unsure about which course the colonies should take when he was summoned to the Virginia Convention in Richmond the following February. The gathering was convened in Richmond because it had become too dangerous for the burgesses to meet in Williamsburg.

Patrick Henry sat beside George in the crowded St. John's Church, where the convention was held. As George glanced at his fellow delegate, he saw a red-haired, strong-jawed lawyer in his late thirties and a firebrand for revolution. Soon Patrick Henry was on his feet calling for a motion to create new militia units and urging that every man in Virginia be drilled to take up arms. When the motion came to a vote, George opposed creating any more military units in Virginia. In his opinion it would look far too much as though Virginia was inviting a war and not merely preparing to defend itself. Other delegates agreed with George's view, and the motion failed.

At that moment Patrick Henry jumped to his feet and stepped into the aisle. In his Scottish brogue he challenged every man sitting in the church. "I repeat it, sir, we must fight. An appeal to arms and to the God of Hosts is all that is left to us. They tell us, sir, that we are weak, unable to cope with so formidable an adversary. But when shall we be stronger? Will it be the next week or the next year?"

George watched in amazement as Patrick Henry fell down on one knee and crossed his wrists as if they were chained together before going on. "There is no retreat but in submission and slavery. Our chains are forged. Their clanking may be heard on the plains of Boston. The war is inevitable. And let it come! I repeat it, sir, let it come!...Gentlemen may cry, peace, peace—but there is no peace. The war is actually begun. The next gale that surveys from the north will bring to our ears the clash of resounding arms. Our brethren are already on the field! Why stand idle here? Is life so dear, or peace so sweet, as to be purchased at the price of chains and slavery? Forbid it, Almighty God!"

Springing back to his feet Patrick Henry then opened his arms wide. "I know not what course others may take, but as for me, give me liberty, or give me death." With that he thrust an imaginary dagger into his chest and sunk back into his seat beside George.

Pandemonium broke out. Some delegates rose to their feet cheering wildly. Others shouted abuse at Patrick Henry, denouncing him as a warmonger. Somewhere in the midst of all this noise, George Washington made a decision. Patrick Henry was right. War was inevitable. Neither King George nor Parliament had done one thing to help resolve the situation in the colonies. In fact, the king had labeled the Continental Congress the "most daring spirit of resistance and disobedience to law." Some members of Parliament had tried to get the harsh Boston Port Act overturned, but they were soundly defeated by a vote of sixty-eight to eighteen. Now, George told himself, it was time to admit the truth— England would not stop taxing the American colonies unfairly until it was forced to do so at the point of a gun. George was not surprised when the following day he was appointed to increase the size of the Virginia militia and create a cavalry.

When the meeting was over, George hurried back to Mount Vernon to tell Martha all the news and to call for volunteer soldiers. As he rode home, he was very aware of the gamble he was taking in contemplating war with England. He and Martha belonged to an elite group of tidewater Virginia society, those with land and money. Now that George was officially a *patriot*, the governor could take everything he owned. George Washington was now a widely known traitor to the British, and if they got their hands on him, he would certainly be deported to London and hanged. It was a sobering reality, and one he did not discuss with Martha. However, he knew she was an intelligent woman and aware of the great risk he was taking.

Back at Mount Vernon there was so much to be done. New volunteers had to be formed into a fighting force, crops had to be planted, and George needed to set his affairs in order before he went off to the Second Continental Congress. He turned oversight of his financial affairs over to his sister Betty's husband, Fielding Lewis, while his cousin Lund Washington, with help from Martha, would run the plantation. He asked his brother Jack to supervise the fishing boats and flour mill.

In the meantime rumors had been circulating, but on April 29, 1775, a messenger came galloping up the lane to Mount Vernon with a report. The details were sketchy, but he told George that in the early hours of April 19 one thousand British soldiers had set out toward Concord and Lexington, Massachusetts, to round up rebels, weapons, ammunition, and two of the leading patriots, Samuel Adams and John Hancock. A volunteer army of minutemen had met them, and a battle had followed. Both British and colonial soldiers had been killed, though apparently the British came off worse. They had retreated to Boston, and the pursuing militia had blockaded all routes out of the town.

George's heart quickened. The first shots had been fired! He was glad the start of the next Continental Congress was only a week away.

That night George discussed the new threat with Martha and talked about his upcoming trip to attend the next session of the Continental Congress. "I'll be back by July," he told Martha as they sat looking out at the Potomac River. He watched as she wiped a tear from her cheek. "You have plenty to do between now and then!" he said in the most carefree voice he could muster.

Martha managed a little smile. "I've invited my mother to visit," she replied. "I do hope she comes. The house is so lonely without you."

George nodded. "Well, I won't be gone long." He did not tell his wife that in his travel trunk was his old army uniform, just in case he got caught up in war while he was away.

A week later George Washington arrived in Philadelphia. The task that awaited the Second Continental Congress was huge. This time John

Hancock was elected as president of the gathering. The debates over what should happen next were endless and complicated, and just as the delegates thought they might be able to agree on something, new information that changed everything trickled in. Two separate groups of militiamen from Vermont and New England, led by Ethan Allen and Benedict Arnold, had seized Fort Ticonderoga from a small garrison of British soldiers. New York Colony became anxious because British troops were marching toward New York City, and New England needed help to supply their militia who were still blockading Boston.

On June 14, a hot and sticky day, the Congress continued to meet. Once again all the windows and doors were tightly locked to prevent loyalist spies from hearing the discussions going on inside. Everyone was seated when John Adams got up to speak. "I raise the call for a grand American army," he began.

Over the shoulder of Thomas Jefferson, George could see John Hancock straighten his back. The corners of Hancock's mouth turned upward.

"And to lead that army," John Adams went on with great drama, "I propose a man who is very well known to all of us, a gentleman whose skill and experience as an officer, whose independent fortune, great talents, and excellent universal character will command the approbation of all America."

George watched as John Hancock began to rise out of his seat.

"And that man is—Colonel George Washington."

John Hancock sat down with a thud, his face purple with indignation that he had not been nominated. George stood up but not to take a bow or address the Congress. No, he was feeling so embarrassed that he gathered his bag and fled the room. He found refuge in a nearby library and refused to go back to the Continental Congress until they had finished discussing his nomination and comparing his leadership abilities with those of John Hancock and other colonial militia leaders who were present.

The following day they were still arguing about who should lead the Continental army, even though there were no soldiers in it yet. George rejoined the group at a local pub for dinner and was greeted by Thomas Jefferson.

"Good evening, General!" Jefferson said, grinning. "Your appointment was unanimous."

Other delegates crowded into the room, and everyone wanted to congratulate George. George, however, did not feel one bit like celebrating. He could barely eat a bite of his dinner. He was too worried about how he was going to do it. How was he going to bring men from thirteen different colonies together to fight as one against the best-equipped and most well-trained army in the world? And if he failed? What then?

The following day George formally accepted the position as commander in chief of the Continental army. He refused to accept a salary because he did not want to profit from the war. All he asked was that the Continental Congress cover his expenses.

That night George wrote a very difficult letter to his wife. He hated to think what Martha would say when she read it. He tried to explain that he could not refuse the position even if he wanted to. He wrote, "I am now set down to write you on a subject which fills me with inexpressible concern and this concern is greatly aggravated and increased when I reflect upon the uneasiness I know it will cause you...But it has been a kind destiny that has thrown me upon this service. I shall hope that my undertaking is designed to answer some good purpose."

George followed his letter to Martha with one to his brother Jack in which he wrote, "I am now to bid adieu to you and every kind of domestic ease for a while. I am embarking on a wide ocean, boundless in its prospect, and from whence, perhaps, no safe harbor is to be found." Along with the letter George included the latest copy of his will. He did not know what lay ahead for him, but he was ready to die in the pursuit of freedom from the tyranny of the English if need be.

Chapter 11

The Continental Army

At dawn on June 23, 1775, forty-three-year-old General George Washington mounted a tall white horse and rode down Second Street in Philadelphia. A band struck up a rousing tune as Charles Lee and Philip Schuyler rode up to join the new commander in chief. Crowds of cheering colonists lined the cobblestone street. George waved to them. Finally, after nearly a week of paperwork and long meetings, he was on his way to Boston to take command of the Massachusetts militia in the name of the Continental army.

As his horse trotted down Old York Road toward the Delaware River, George tried to put the endless bickering over who should be made generals and officers in the new army behind him. Many delegates to the Continental Congress did not care who was the best equipped for the job. They wanted men from their home colonies to fill as many top posts as possible. Eventually four major generals were appointed: Philip Schuyler of New York; Charles Lee of Virginia; and Artemus Ward and Israel Putman, both from Massachusetts, who were already in Boston leading the militia. In George's opinion they were not the best men for the job, but he resigned himself to work with them anyway.

Behind George rode his two aides, Thomas Mifflin and Joseph Reed. George was pleased with these two young men from Philadelphia. He had chosen them himself, and they were both smart and well educated.

Once the crowd was left behind, George, his aides, and the two generals transferred to a carriage for the long, dusty trip to Boston. They had plenty to talk about. The night before, an exhausted messenger had arrived to tell the Congress that the Boston militia had won a great battle against the British at Bunker Hill. This gave the colonists the high ground above Boston and an ideal position from which to bombard ships. This information made George want to get to Boston as quickly as possible. If it was true, perhaps the British could be forced out of Boston in a week or two and Parliament would come to its senses, pardon the colonists who had dared to stand up to them, and grant the colonies the right to have a say in their own taxes. It was a wonderful prospect. George might be back at Mount Vernon by fall!

When the group arrived in New York, George's hopes were dashed. The messenger who had rushed to Philadelphia to tell the Congress about the Boston militia's victory at Bunker Hill had left before the battle was over. Now George was hearing the whole story.

An eyewitness to the entire day's events told George that during the night the Boston militia had crept along the Charlestown Neck. Under cover of darkness they set up a fort on the top of a hill called Breed's Hill, which was behind the city of Charlestown. When the British woke in Boston the following morning, they saw colonial troops looking straight across the Charles River at them. Soon the British were firing at them from Copp's Hill in Boston. A few hours later fifteen hundred redcoats were put ashore at the bottom of Breed's Hill. With bayonets gleaming, they charged up the hill, and a ferocious fight ensued. Two more waves of redcoats followed, and when the smoke finally cleared that afternoon, the British had gained control of Breed's Hill, Bunker Hill, and the rest of the Charlestown Neck. But they had paid a heavy price for their victory. Rebel spies who were among the two thousand loyalists who stayed in Boston informed the patriot Colonel Prescott that 226 British soldiers lay dead and 2,400 were wounded. The Boston militia, who officially "lost" the battle, lost far fewer men. One hundred forty rebels were killed, 270 wounded, and thirty taken prisoner.

The more George heard, the glummer he became. It was obvious that the British were not going to give up their colonies without a bloody fight. Could the untrained and ill-equipped colonials prevail against the most powerful empire on earth? And if it were possible, did he really know enough about warfare to lead them?

Sobered by the news, George traveled on toward Boston the following day. He had other things to concern himself about besides the rebels' loss at Bunker Hill. Canada was a particularly perplexing question. Fourteen years before, George had fought for the British and been overjoyed when they had won Canada from the French. Now he was not so enthusiastic about having British neighbors. Since Canada, in effect, was the fourteenth British colony in North America, George and many other members of the Continental Congress wondered whether its citizens might want to join in a rebellion against the "mother" country. After all, the new Quebec Act had taken away the right of Canadians to have a trial by jury or to have any say at all in selecting their governor or ruling council members.

The Continental Congress decided that General Schuyler should lead an effort to free Canada from British rule so that the citizens there could join forces with the rest of the colonies. Before leaving New York, George worked out a plan whereby General Schuyler would put together a patriot army and attack Montreal and Quebec before the British had time to strengthen their troops in those cities. George went over the details of the plan with Philip Schuyler before sending him off to "liberate" their northern neighbor.

On Sunday, July 2, General George Washington arrived in Cambridge, Massachusetts, in the middle of a rainstorm. Early the next morning he was out inspecting "his" men. Things did not go well from the start. George's first question regarding how many men were in the Massachusetts camp was met with a shrug of the shoulders. No one knew for sure. There were men from many different militias, and their leaders could not cooperate long enough to add up how many men they had altogether. The next question showed an even bigger weakness in George's new army. George asked how much gunpowder was in the storerooms. He was relieved to hear there were 308 barrels, until he asked to see them. When the barrels were actually counted, there were only 36!

When he found this out, George tried hard to control his temper. How could he command an army of an unknown number of men whose leaders could not work together, and with thirty-six barrels of gunpowder? Things had to change fast.

George suspected the British would stay put in Boston, not risking another battle like Bunker Hill, until more troops arrived from England. Thankfully, he was right, and this gave him enough time to whip the new Continental army into shape. And whip them he did. A list of basic military rules was posted. The list included rules against cursing, drunkenness, stealing, leaving camp without permission, skipping chapel time, and using the areas in front of the tents as an open toilet. The soldiers who did not obey these rules were whipped up to five hundred lashes in front of their comrades.

The atmosphere in the camp changed rapidly. Regimental leaders reported the number of men under their command to George, and the total added up to sixteen thousand, two thousand of whom were injured or too ill to fight. The fourteen thousand men who were fit were put to work digging toilet trenches, laying paths, and constructing a ten-mile-long palisade.

Although it pleased George to see the men working, he soon grew restless. Waiting around for British reinforcements to arrive and spying on the redcoats, who were spying back on them, was no way to win a war! The rebel army had to do something.

George called his generals to a council of war and outlined a plan that had been forming in his head for some time. "Now is the time to strike the British," he said, thumping the table they were all seated around. "We have more men than they, and they are running out of food. I say we attack Boston before Christmas! Winter is coming, and I do not have the supplies to outfit our soldiers in winter clothes, nor are their tents sufficient to keep them warm. Besides, many of the men only enlisted until December 31, when they will go home, taking their rifles with them. Unless they see some action, I doubt many of them will want to sign up again, and it is proving very hard to attract new recruits."

When the plan was put to a vote, only one general, Charles Lee, agreed with George. Everyone else thought they should wait until word came back as to how the British Parliament had reacted to news of Bunker Hill. Surely, the other generals argued, the British would see that the colonists were serious about their rights and would give in to their demands.

George was not so sure they would, and he did have the right to override the vote and invade Boston anyway. But he chose not to. Either the Continental army would attack as a united force, or it would not attack at all.

After the meeting with his generals, George wrote to Martha apologizing for the fact that he would not be home in time for Christmas as he had hoped. Instead, he invited Martha to join him in Cambridge if she felt up to the long trip.

All George could do now was organize the men into building barracks and hold on to the snippets of hopeful news that General Schuyler was sending back to him. General Schuyler was staying in Albany, New York, where he was overseeing the training and supplying of his troops. While General Schuyler's men were being outfitted for battle, Schuyler's subordinate, General Richard Montgomery, was already out fighting with his band of soldiers. Their plans were going well, and they captured a string of British forts as they made their way north toward Montreal.

There was more positive news in September, when the Continental Congress announced that colonial ships were allowed to attack and overrun any British ship they came across. The cargo was to be divided between the colonial captain and Congress, with the ship itself becoming a part of the Continental fleet. Although it would have been suicide for a captain to attack ships in Boston Harbor, a few British ships bringing military supplies from the naval base at Halifax were captured. George was delighted to receive 2,000 muskets, 100,000 flints, 20,000 rounds of shot, and 30 musketballs—all courtesy of King George III!

This capture did not solve all of George's weapons problems. Every day as he stared through his eyeglass, he could see the huge iron cannons that the British had. If the Continental army had cannons, it could blast the British out of Boston. But where could it get cannons? Then George had a daring idea.

When the British fled from Fort Ticonderoga and Crown Point, they had left many cannons behind—cannons George could use to bombard Boston. There was just one problem: the cannons were more than 150 miles away. It would take a superhuman effort to transport them over the Berkshire Mountains in winter. However, George thought that one man might just be able to do it: a man named Henry Knox, a twenty-five-year-old bookstore owner from Boston who was fascinated with guns, cannons, and other weapons. From the first day that volunteers were called for, Knox had been fighting for the patriot cause and had quickly risen to the rank of colonel in charge of artillery (even though there was very little of it to be in charge of). Colonel Putman vouched for Knox's commitment to the patriot cause, even though his wife's father was an official in the British government and her entire family were staunch loyalists.

The end of October brought sobering news. In his annual speech to Parliament, King George III had slammed the door on any idea of reforming the colonial laws. In fact, he declared the American colonies in open rebellion and promised to recruit professional fighting troops from Russia or Germany to crush the colonies. The hope of a peaceful settlement was growing dim.

On December 11, 1775, a carriage bearing the Washington coat of arms pulled up to George's headquarters at Vassall House. Inside were Martha, Jacky, and Jacky's wife, Nelly. George hurried out to meet them.

"You should have seen the fuss they made over us in Philadelphia!" Martha told her husband. "There was so much pomp you would have thought I was a great somebody!"

George smiled, although he reminded himself that today's heroes can easily turn into tomorrow's scapegoats. And he was going to do everything in his power to stop that from happening.

Chapter 12

Victory and Defeat

George Washington stood looking out the window at the gray February sky. "I'm of the opinion that we have to do it," he said, turning to face General Israel Putnam. "What do you think?"

Israel Putnam shook his head, "It's quiet a gamble," he replied. "First we have to build a fort on top of Dorchester Heights without the British noticing us. Then we have to man it with soldiers who do not even have a musket apiece when the redcoats storm the hill."

George sighed. "But what is the alternative? So many of the soldiers have lost heart since they heard how the British beat us back from Canada at New Year's. We have the cannons now, and if we don't make some kind of mark soon, Parliament will think they have us beaten."

"If you think it's the right thing to do, then you have my vote," General Putnam replied. "After what the British did to my men on Bunker Hill, I'd like to get a bit of my own back on them."

"Then we'll begin on March first," George decided. "It's time to show the British what a few rebels can do!"

During the next week, George and his officers spent many hours huddled over war plans. Every detail was discussed, every possibility covered. Once the details were agreed upon, the men got to work. Soldiers began building large frames from lumber that would be dragged into place on Dorchester Heights and filled with hay and covered with sacking and dirt.

Connected to the mainland by a narrow neck of land that was blockaded by the Continental militia, Boston was virtually an island. If the patriots succeeded in occupying Dorchester Heights, the British would be surrounded, and their ships in the harbor, which supplied and protected the troops in the city, would be within easy range of Continental cannons.

By March 1 everything was ready. To cover the noise of thousands of soldiers, carts, horses, and oxen moving the barricades into place, the cannons that Henry Knox had brought from Fort Ticonderoga opened fire. They fired for two nights to lull the British holed up in Boston. Finally, on the night of March 4, George gave the order for the men to move out.

It was a dark, moonless night, and as the cannons reverberated through the darkness, thousands of soldiers crept forward, tugging the giant wooden frames behind them. They maneuvered the frames into place on the slopes of Dorchester Heights overlooking Boston. Once the frames were in place, other soldiers filled them with bales of hay while still others covered the hay with mounds of dirt. An hour before dawn the cannons were pulled into place along the barricade.

As dawn broke that morning, George knew the British would scarcely believe their eyes. The patriots had built a fortification overnight.

George watched through his telescope as the British troops assembled and barges and small boats moved in to ferry the men across Boston Harbor. He assumed that British Major General William Howe was going to attack and try to take back the high ground.

As the British marshaled their troops for the attack, a vicious storm blew in. Rain pelted down, and the wind churned up the harbor, scattering the boats assembled to transport the soldiers. George decided that William Howe must have had second thoughts about the attack while the storm raged, because when the heavy rain stopped washing over Boston and the wind ceased whipping up the water in the harbor, the British began preparing to abandon the city. George watched in amazement

On St. Patrick's Day, March 17, 1776, the last of the overloaded British ships sailed out of Boston

Harbor. George Washington became an instant hero. He was granted an honorary degree from Harvard College, and the Continental Congress had a special gold coin struck in his honor. George hardly had time to get excited about any of this. He was sure he hadn't seen the last of General Howe. After they regrouped, probably in Halifax, Nova Scotia, the British would be back, maybe not to Boston, but somewhere along the coast. And as he studied the map, George became convinced that that place would be New York City.

There was something else George concluded as he studied the map—New York City would be virtually impossible for patriot troops to defend. It was surrounded on three sides by water, and Manhattan Island, on which the city stood, was long and narrow. Since George did not have enough men to position along the island's entire coastline, it would be relatively easy for the British to find a place to come ashore and attack New York from the rear, surrounding it and trapping the entire Continental army. George could see only one solution: New York should be abandoned and burned to the ground!

When George suggested this to the Continental Congress, his idea was met with shock and disbelief. How could the Congress order a city to be razed? How would such an action win over the thousands of colonials who had not made up their minds whether they were patriots or loyalists? George knew they were right from a political point of view, but he was a military man and assured them that even though he would do his best, there was no way to keep New York safe.

On July 9, 1776, George rode into New York City. Martha was by his side. She had surprised him with her courage by insisting on remaining with him and the troops. It was a day of strange contrasts. On the one hand, in the harbor a forest of masts greeted George. The British had arrived five days earlier and were now stationed on Staten Island. Thirty-nine thousand men under the command of Major General William Howe, whom George had chased out of Boston, were poised to attack New York City. On the other hand, a courier delivered a most amazing piece of paper. When George read what was written on it, he called for it to be read aloud from the balcony of city hall at the foot of Broadway.

George sat on horseback, a short distance from the gathering crowd. A gong sounded to quiet everyone, and then a man started reading.

In Congress, July 4, 1776. A Declaration by the Representatives of the United States of America, in General Congress assembled. When in the course of human events, it becomes necessary for one people to dissolve the political bands which have connected them with another, and to assume among the powers of the earth, the separate and equal station to which the laws of nature and of nature's God entitle them, a decent respect to the opinions of mankind

requires that they should declare the causes
which impel them to the separation.

George watched as everyone stood spellbound,
waiting to hear what was coming next. Even the
babies in the audience were hushed.

We hold these truths to be self-evident,
that all men are created equal, that they are
endowed by their Creator with certain
unalienable rights, that among these are
life, liberty and the pursuit of happiness...

A cheer went up from the crowd, and then the
reading continued. When the reading of the
Declaration of Independence was over, the crowd
stood silent for a moment. Then someone shouted,
"Tear down the coat of arms."

The crowd sprang into action. Several men
hoisted boys onto their shoulders, and the boys
grabbed for King George's coat of arms that hung
over the door of city hall and pulled it to the ground.

"The statue," someone else yelled, and the crowd
wheeled around in unison and raced down the
street toward Bowling Green, where a statue of the
king on horseback stood. Within minutes both men
and women were attacking the statue with whatever they had in their hands. Several hours later
the statue was hauled away to be melted down into
forty-two thousand bullets for the patriot cause.

That night a candle shone in the window of
every patriot home in the city. Independence fever

ran high—in everyone except George Washington. He thought the document was wonderful, but he was aware that his troops could be snuffed out just as easily as any of the candles burning to celebrate the Declaration of Independence. It was one thing to declare independence. It was quite another to bring it to pass in the thirteen colonies. George was certain the British would not give up so easily on America.

Indeed, the British had no intention of allowing the rebels to hold on to New York. William Howe's troops crossed New York Harbor and were deployed on Long Island. On August 27, the British and the Continental army faced off against each other. It was a pitched battle, but in the end the patriot army was forced to retreat. The following night, under the cover of heavy fog, George Washington and twelve thousand Continental soldiers were able to escape across the East River to Manhattan Island, avoiding certain capture by the British.

On Manhattan, George arranged his men to defend the island as best they could. On September 15, 1776, the British crossed the East River and attacked Manhattan Island. They came ashore at Kip's Bay midway up the island and had a free run to capture the city of New York, since the Connecticut militia unit protecting Kip's Bay had fled in confusion and fear. George was furious at the men's cowardice. How would he ever win the war against the British if his men fled in battle?

The following day, the Connecticut militia redeemed itself in the battle of Harlem Heights, fending off a British attack. This time George commended them for their bravery under fire.

Instead of pushing forward, the British decided to stop temporarily and build fortifications across the northern end of Manhattan Island to protect the city from any rebel counterattack. While they worked, someone set the city on fire behind them. Only a wind shift saved the whole city from being burned to the ground. As it was, 493 houses were destroyed in the blaze.

Finally, as the British wrapped up work on their fortifications, George realized he could not hold on to New York City and it was pointless to try. On October 16 he ordered the Continental army to retreat off Manhattan Island. New York City was now firmly in the hands of the British.

The British, however, were not content to have just recaptured New York. They wanted to rout George Washington and his Continental army, capture Philadelphia, the rebel capital, and bring a quick end to the rebellion, putting the colonies firmly back under the control of King George and Parliament.

Feeling they had the upper hand, the British army set out to pursue the Continental army. During November British General Charles Cornwallis swept across New Jersey, capturing Newark, New Brunswick, Perth Amboy, Princeton, Trenton, and Bordentown. It was all George and his army could do to stay ahead of the British as they scurried from village to village.

Finally, on December 7, George Washington and his men were able to escape across the Delaware River into Pennsylvania just ahead of the redcoats. General Cornwallis decided not to pursue them across the river but rather to set up winter camp in New Jersey. They would finish routing the rebels in the spring.

As if this were not enough for George to be concerned about, at the same time he was fleeing across the Delaware, General Henry Clinton and his redcoats had captured Newport, Rhode Island, for the British.

A spy reported to George that the British, fresh from their victories, were boasting they would finish "lickin'" the Americans in the spring.

George knew he had to do something before then, but what?

Chapter 13

Patriot Victories

Geoorge Washington stood in his tent studying a map of the northeast. Spies had informed him that British and Hessian soldiers were wintering over at five small towns across the Delaware in western New Jersey. He knew it would be impossible for the Continental army to wage an all-out assault on New York City or Newport, Rhode Island, but it might just be possible to attack one or two of these winter outposts. There was just one problem. The farmers in the area where the British were holed up were almost all loyalists. They tacked red ribbons to their doors to show their loyalty. It would be impossible for patriot soldiers to march more than a mile into New Jersey before one of the local farmers rode off to warn the redcoats. It seemed as if there was nothing that could be done—until the snow fell and the Hessian troops stationed at Trenton began to get bored.

The Hessians were German mercenary troops retained by King George to help bring England's wayward North American colonies back into line. However, the Hessians stationed at Trenton began making forays out into the surrounding farmland. And instead of acting like an army representing the King of England, the Germans broke into houses, stealing or smashing everything they could find. They attacked groups of women and girls, until the loyalist farmers were terrified of the very army that was supposed to protect them against the "rebels."

Slowly public opinion began to turn. Every day more and more farmers sent word to George Washington that they were changing sides. They were ready to do whatever they could to support the Americans. Many farmers began forming their own militia groups and ambushing Hessian patrols, killing two or three soldiers a day. But this was not enough to make much of an impact on the troops. Something much more significant had to be done to show the English that the rebels still believed in their cause. Such action would also bolster the flagging spirits of the patriot fighters after the rout at New York and retreat across New Jersey.

George knew that if he acted at all, it would have to be quickly, since the soldiers' enlistments expired on New Year's Day. For the second year in a row, he would have to recruit a new army.

It was one of George's best officers, Benedict Arnold, who came up with the plan. He suggested that the rebels make a daring attack on Trenton. The attack would take place early on December 26, hoping that the Hessians would be tired after a day and night of holiday partying. According to the plan, patriot soldiers would cross the Delaware River and attack Trenton from three sides.

At two in the afternoon of December 25, 1776, at McKonkey's Ferry on the edge of the Delaware River, George Washington mounted his tall chestnut horse and gave the order to move out. Nine-foot-wide and sixty-foot-long iron ore barges loaded with men, cannons, and horses were rowed out from the riverbank. Skillfully, those rowing the boats maneuvered them among the ice floes that clogged the river.

The men aboard the barges were still wearing summer clothes, since the Continental army had no winter uniforms to issue them. They slapped themselves with folded arms and stamped their feet to try to keep warm. Many of the men's shoes were so worn that they had packed them with paper to cover the holes in the soles. And the men wore blankets for capes. They were a ragtag bunch, but George believed they were up to the challenge of routing the Hessians.

Before they set out, George wanted to give the men something to take with them. However, there were no extra rations to spare. Instead he ordered his commanders to read an essay to the men:

These are the times that try men's souls. The summer soldier and the sunshine patriot will, in this crisis, shrink from the service of his country; but he that stands it *now*, deserves the love and thanks of man and woman. Tyranny, like hell, is not easily conquered; yet we have this consolation with us, that the harder the conflict, the more glorious the triumph.

Thomas Paine, a journalist who was busy writing essays to inspire the patriot cause, had penned the words. George hoped the stirring words would inspire his men in battle because there were no plans for retreat. He expected every man to fight to the end. Indeed, the password for the operation was "Victory or Death."

George Washington was the first across the river. In the midst of the blizzard that had blown up and howled around him, he took a seat on a crate and waited quietly, talking to and encouraging his men from time to time.

It was four in the morning before all twenty-four hundred men plus cannons and equipment had been ferried across the river. For this fight George had committed his entire army. He had held back no reserves in case the plan did not work out. It was a gamble, but one George felt he could win. And if he won, he believed the victory would revive the spirits of patriots everywhere in the cause of independence.

Once on the New Jersey side of the river, the men fell into formation and began the ten-mile march to Trenton. It was bitter cold as the men marched. The blizzard hurled snow in their faces, and many of the men left bloody footprints in the snow because of their worn-out shoes. Exhausted, two soldiers sat down by the side of the road and froze to death in the icy wind.

Before they reached Trenton, George divided up his men to attack the city from three sides. At exactly eight o'clock on the morning of December 26, George Washington gave the order to attack. Gunfire exploded on Trenton.

The Hessian soldiers were taken completely by surprise. Most of them, including their commanding officer, Colonel Johann Rall, were still sleeping off a day of Christmas revelry, just as George had hoped. Groggy German soldiers scrambled out of bed, threw on coats and pants, grabbed their rifles, and stumbled out into the street. Many of them didn't even have time to pull on their boots. They ran about in the icy snow-covered streets in their socks.

In the streets, grapeshot fired from cannons at both ends of the town cut the Hessians down. Panicked, the men bolted, running down side streets, where they were met by patriot soldiers and their bayonets.

Colonel Rall, a man universally hated by all in Trenton, jumped onto his horse and galloped up and down the street trying to get his men formed into ranks to fight back. His efforts were fruitless. His frightened men ignored his orders and tried to flee Trenton. Within a few minutes two shots pierced Johann Rall, who bled profusely as two of his men dragged him from his horse and carried his wounded body into the town's Methodist church.

Bayonet-wielding Continental soldiers pursued most of the Hessians who managed to flee Trenton. The last of the terrified Germans surrendered after being cornered while trying to cross a boggy creek.

George couldn't have been happier. His plan had worked better than he had imagined. Taken completely by surprise, the Hessian soldiers had been routed. "Major Wilkerson, this is a glorious day for our country," George said to one of his subordinates.

"Do we go on to Princeton?" the major asked.

It was a good question. Although George wanted to march on Princeton, after conferring with his officers, he learned that the fifteen hundred men from the Philadelphia division had not shown up for the battle, and so they could not reinforce the Continental army for the attack on Princeton. As well, a number of the German soldiers had managed to elude capture. By now they would be halfway to Princeton to warn the British troops garrisoned there for the winter. So even though only four of his men had been killed in the battle, George decided to turn back. Given the condition of his men in the atrocious weather, he did not relish attacking a force of British soldiers who would know they were coming and had had time to entrench themselves for battle. Princeton would have to wait for another day.

George ordered his men back across the Delaware River. They took with them the 948 Hessian soldiers they had captured. However, getting back across the river, which had iced up further, was no easy task, and three more men froze to death along the way.

From the Continental army's camp beside the Delaware River, the Hessian prisoners were marched to Philadelphia to be locked up. It was just the morale boost the Americans needed. People poured into the street to watch the bedraggled Germans as they marched past. Soon news of the patriot victory at the Battle of Trenton spread throughout the colonies.

George was furious when he learned that the Philadelphia militia had not shown up for the battle because their commanders assumed it was impossible to attack in a blizzard. He was even angrier when he received word on December 27 that the militia were finally in place for the battle. Their commanders had no idea that the battle had already been fought and the Continental army had won and returned back across the river. Now George had fifteen hundred men stranded in New Jersey, and the British were sure to bring in reinforcements and try to strike back. There was only one thing to do: he would have to cross the river again, rescue the militia, and strike Princeton before reinforcements arrived.

In planning this, George again faced the problem that his men's enlistments would expire on December 31 and that almost every soldier in the army was planning to return home. Finally George ordered that the men be lined up in regiments. The men stood at attention facing George, who was mounted on his horse. George spoke to them about the battle at Trenton and what a great victory it had been. And he told them of future battles they could win if only the men would reenlist in the army. When he was finished speaking, George rode to one side and invited the men who wanted to reenlist to step forward. A drumroll sounded, but not one man made a move.

Embarrassed that no one had stepped forward, George wheeled his horse around and began to address his men again. "You have done all I asked you to do, and more than could be reasonably expected. But your country is at stake...You have worn yourselves out with fatigues and hardships, but we know not how to spare you. If you will consent to stay only one month longer, you render that service to the cause of liberty and to your country which you probably never can do under any other circumstance. Today we face the crisis which is to decide our destiny."

As he spoke, George rode up and down the ranks of men, looking them in the eye. This time as the drumroll sounded, men began to step forward, until twelve hundred men had reenlisted.

George Washington and his army once again crossed the Delaware River into New Jersey and made camp. On January 2, 1777, as the commanding officers made plans for their attack on Princeton, British General Cornwallis, with eight thousand troops, cornered the Continental soldiers on one side of the Assunpick River east of Trenton.

The situation seemed desperate. General Cornwallis's men far outnumbered George's. If Cornwallis chose to attack, he could easily rout the Continental army and capture its general. But the British did something George had noticed them doing during the fighting in New York. When they had the advantage, they rarely used it. Instead of pursuing the defeated patriot army when they had the upper hand, they made camp and resumed the fight the next day or several days later. It was this behavior that had allowed the Continental army to escape the clutches of the British in New York. And now General Cornwallis was doing the same thing. Instead of moving in to destroy the Continental army while he had the advantage, he chose to make camp and attack in the morning.

George decided to exploit this British weakness. He ordered his men to noisily begin digging trenches and to light huge bonfires. To the British it would seem as if the American soldiers were preparing for battle in the morning. Indeed they were, but not with General Cornwallis's men.

In the early hours of January 3, as the bonfires burned brightly, the Continental forces crept out of camp by a back road and made their way around the flank of General Cornwallis's forces. To muffle the sound of the troops on the move, the wheels of the wagons and cannons were wrapped in blankets.

The plan did not, however, immediately go well for the American fighters. Just before dawn they encountered a contingent of crack British troops on their way to reinforce General Cornwallis's forces. The British forces mounted a bayonet charge at the Americans, who scattered in the face of it.

Seeing his men in danger of being routed before they reached Princeton, George galloped into the middle of the skirmish. He exhorted and cajoled his troops back into line, and mounted on his horse, he led the men, with their bayonets fixed, into battle. When they were within range, he ordered the men to halt and fire. Two volleys of gunfire rang out, and smoke filled the air. When it cleared, George was still on his horse urging his men forward. Now they had the upper hand on the British troops and began to pursue them until the redcoats turned and ran.

As the American forces approached Princeton, seeing what had just happened, the British soldiers manning the barricades fled into Nassau Hall at the College of New Jersey (now Princeton University). The solid stone building should have been easy for the British to defend, but by now the British soldiers were scared and cowered inside. When a cannon ball from an American six-pound field gun crashed through the stone wall of the building and troops stormed the front door, the British inside threw down their weapons and surrendered. George Washington and his men had captured Princeton from the British.

After its victory at Princeton, the Continental army made its way to Morristown, where it camped while the British army fled. On January 6 American troops took control of Hackensack and Elizabeth-town. Now all the British controlled in New Jersey was Perth Amboy and New Brunswick.

George Washington was satisfied with his victories and was glad his troops were able to settle in at Morristown and rest. While the men rested, George busied himself recruiting more soldiers. By spring 1777 he had eight thousand troops.

In June news came that British General Howe had pulled all of his troops back to New York and Staten Island. George knew he would not be doing this unless he had a plan. Was he intending to march his troops up the Hudson River to meet the British force under General John Burgoyne marching down from Quebec? Or did he intend to put the men on ships and take them to a new battlefront. And if so, where would that be? Philadelphia? Charleston? Wherever it was, the American troops did not have ships to travel on. They would have to march to meet the British wherever they decided to fight next.

George decided to wait until he had more information before he made his next move. On July 23 he got part of the answer. Seventeen thousand British troops were loaded into 260 warships that sailed out of New York Bay. But where were they headed? George would have to wait some more to find out, and that was something he didn't like to do.

Chapter 14

A Cold Winter

George Washington wrote that he was "in the most perfect ignorance, and disagreeable state of suspense" as he waited for news of where General Howe was going to land his men. While he waited, however, George had to contend with the twelve thousand British soldiers under General John Burgoyne's command. In their march south from Quebec these soldiers had easily overrun the patriot forces at Fort Ticonderoga on June 15. To combat General Burgoyne and his men, George had sent two generals, Benedict Arnold and Horatio Gates, north to join Major General Philip Schuyler in an attempt to prevent the British from moving farther south.

Finally, frustrated with waiting for word on General Howe's whereabouts, George set out for

Philadelphia to bring Congress up-to-date on his latest decisions. He arrived on August 1, 1777, and went straight to Congress, where he heard something that annoyed him nearly as much as waiting for word of where the British were headed. Congress had voted that a nineteen-year-old Frenchman named Marie Joseph Motier, the Marquis de Lafayette, be given the rank of major general and assigned to George Washington's care.

Don't I have enough to do without baby-sitting a pampered French boy? George fumed to himself when he was told the details of Lafayette's new appointment. It was becoming all too common now. Although the French had not joined the United States and declared war on Britain, more and more Frenchmen, and indeed men from other European countries, were "showing up" to help the Americans win the war. Most of them had fought in various wars in Europe, though they exaggerated both their ranks and their success. Most of them spoke no English and wanted to be placed in command over American troops with whom they could not even communicate. Not surprisingly, this made the European officers in the Continental army very unpopular! And now an idealistic nineteen-year-old who had married into one of the three richest families in France and been given a captaincy in the French army was to be entrusted into George's care.

Several members of Congress explained to George that they had given Lafayette the high rank of major general in the hope that he might be able to help influence France to join them in their war—provided he was not killed in battle. So along with all of his other problems, George now had to make the young man feel like a soldier without actually exposing him to too much danger because, apart from everything else, his fifteen-year-old wife back in France was pregnant and his father-in-law wanted him back in one piece.

Given how he felt, George was surprised to find himself actually liking "General" Lafayette. Indeed, he liked him a lot. The tall, skinny redhead with a hooked nose was not arrogant like many of the other foreign officers, and he seemed willing to learn from George rather than tell him what to do. By the time news arrived on August 30, 1777, that the British fleet had been sighted off Cape May at the entrance to Delaware Bay, George had welcomed Lafayette under his wing.

Realizing that the British were intending to attack Philadelphia, George sent orders for his 11,500 troops to march to Philadelphia by the shortest route. It was a proud day when General Washington, with General Lafayette at his side, led the Continental army's march through Philadelphia. Most members of Congress had never actually seen the army, and George tried hard to make his men look as professional and powerful as possible. The men marched twelve abreast in a continuous column through the city.

As George tried to devise plans to counter the British attack, he was mystified when word reached him that after entering Delaware Bay, the British fleet had turned around and sailed out to sea again. Was it some kind of trick General Howe was playing, trying to throw the Continental army off balance? George wished he knew.

As George and his officers puzzled over what to do next, word came that the British were putting their troops ashore at Head of Elk, at the northern end of Chesapeake Bay, sixty miles south of Philadelphia. Quickly George marched his troops twenty-five miles south of the city to Brandywine Creek, where he planned to ambush the British as they marched northward.

The plan might have worked if George had known that there were several places along Brandywine Creek where the banks sloped gently down to the water's edge, allowing the river to be easily forded. Because of some misunderstandings in reports, and because George himself did not double-check the information as he usually did, the patriot army positioned itself at only one cross-ing, called Chadd's Ford.

The men waited tensely until September 11, when spies spotted the British coming. Everyone took up positions for the ambush. At first things went well, that is, until the Americans realized that they were about to be ambushed themselves by a large battalion of redcoat soldiers who had crossed the river upstream and crept around behind them.

Thankfully, it was late afternoon when the British outflanked the Americans, and soon dark-ness stopped the fighting. When each side tallied up the dead, wounded, and captured from the battle,

1,200 patriot soldiers had been caught or killed, whereas the British losses amounted to 583 men.

Still George did not feel beaten, nor did his men. As they slept out in the open that night, George was gratified to hear his men encouraging one another with, "All right, boys, we'll do better another time!"

Lafayette had proved brave and useful in the battle, too. He had kept fighting to the very end, and only then did he allow his boot, which was overflowing with blood, to be removed and his leg examined. A bullet had grazed him, and George made a special visit to the hospital tent to see him. He told the doctor, "Treat that boy as if he were my own son."

The two armies were ready in a matter of days to fight again. George tried to lure General Howe into another ambush, and he suspected General Howe was trying to do the same to him. As small skirmishes broke out all around Philadelphia, members of Congress packed up their important papers, burned the rest, and headed west to York, Pennsylvania. Seeing the Congress fleeing, one third of the population hurriedly packed up and fled the city as well.

On September 25 the British captured Philadelphia without firing a shot. However, no sooner had they entered the city than George began making plans to retaliate. On October 4 he struck Germantown, a British outpost seven miles from Philadelphia. The attack was supposed to be a surprise attack like the attack on Trenton, but a thick fog set in and everything went wrong. In the confusion, various American regiments, who could not see clearly, began to fire on each other! In the end the Continental troops were forced to retreat.

Now George was discouraged. He was trying to work out what to do next when, on October 18, an express rider galloped into camp. He carried with him the best possible news. British General John Burgoyne and his entire army had surrendered at Saratoga, New York! Benedict Arnold had led two successful campaigns against them, until the British force was so crippled it gave up the fight.

George immediately sent a fresh rider off to the Congress. The sooner Benjamin Franklin, who was in France, got word of this victory, the sooner he might be able to persuade the French to join in the war.

For now, though, George had to find somewhere for his army to winter over. He led the men westward, just as the mild fall weather turned to sleet and snow.

On December 18 the troops halted on a hill overlooking a valley. In the valley was the village of Valley Forge and the ruins of an iron forge the British had recently destroyed. Beyond the village was a wooded slope about two miles long that George selected for his winter camp. Although the site was exposed to the icy winter wind that now howled through the valley, it was easily defended. It was also only eighteen miles from Philadelphia, close enough for George to keep watch on General Howe and his men.

The first job to be done at the camp was to build sixteen-foot-long by fourteen-foot-wide log cabins for the men to live in. George offered a twelve-dollar prize to the first unit in each regiment to build the best log cabin. The men got to work, and soon the hillside sported cabin-lined streets.

The cabins had earth floors and roofs of straw and dirt, and paper dipped in pig's fat was nailed across the windows to keep out some of the wind while letting in light. The cabins also had mud fireplaces and a chimney.

Despite the protection of the cabins, the men felt the bitter cold. Most of their clothes were now rags, and often the men had to borrow each other's trousers and jackets when it was their turn to go out on guard duty. As well, most of the wood they had to burn was green, which filled the cabins with choking smoke. To add to these discomforts, food was in short supply. The men had no meat to eat, and they survived on "fire-cake," a mixture of flour, water, and salt that was baked on a flat stone in front of the fire.

Given the rugged conditions and their weakened health, many of the men succumbed to various diseases. Pneumonia and malnutrition claimed the lives of a number of men. Scabies, a contagious disease caused when mites burrowed into the men's skin, was a constant irritant. The open sores the disease produced became unbearably itchy, pushing men to the edge of their endurance.

George was concerned about the condition of his men. He wrote letters to the Continental Congress and the legislatures of the various colonies, and the reply was always the same. The Congress and the legislatures wanted independence, yes, but they wanted to win it as cheaply as possible. As a result they were not prepared to send food or money to the Continental army. George fumed at their shortsightedness, especially as he watched more of his men die each day.

To make matters worse, 1777 had been a good harvest for farmers in the area. However, many of these farmers chose to hoard their crops in an attempt to drive up prices. And if that weren't enough, some farmers were supplying the British in Philadelphia with food. General Howe was paying them for their produce in gold, which was worth something, unlike the paper money the Continental army wanted to pay them with.

By February 1778, when George thought he could not endure watching his men suffer anymore, three bright spots appeared on the horizon. The first was that General Nathanael Greene, whom George had made quartermaster, was making great strides in solving the food supply problem. The enterprising Rhode Islander did whatever was necessary to get the food the men desperately needed. Those farmers known to be hoarding goods had them confiscated, were fined, and spent a week locked up in a cold prison. Those caught trading with the British were given 250 lashes on their bare back. By late February wagons were rolling into camp each day laden with supplies.

The second bright spot was the annual winter visit of Martha Washington. Martha confided in George that her heart pounded every time she heard a shot, but she still visited her husband and "her boys," as she called the soldiers, every winter. She brought with her socks and scarves that patriotic Virginia women had knitted for the men, along with a kind word and a motherly smile. Everyone was cheered up by her presence, especially George. Her visits reminded him that there was a quiet, tranquil life waiting for him if the war ever ended.

The third bright spot was also a visitor, a German by the name of Friedrich Wilhelm Augustin Heinrich Ferdinand, Baron von Steuben. The baron had a letter of introduction from Benjamin Franklin, whom he had met in Paris, and he represented himself as a former lieutenant general in the army of Frederick the Great. He spoke no English, only German and French. While George doubted Baron von Steuben's credentials, he recognized that the man had a gift for training soldiers. And that was just what the Continental army needed. If the patriots were to prevail against the British, they needed to be better trained in how to get and stay in battle formation and attack, rather than hiding behind barricades waiting for the enemy to come to them, as they so often did. Baron von Steuben taught the men how to overcome their fear of death, a natural fear among soldiers, and to take pride in their military prowess. In weeklong training sessions, groups of men went through intense training learning various battle formations and how to fight to win.

George was pleased with the progress von Steuben had made with the men. His men were now the fighting force he had hoped they would be, and he was eager to test them in battle.

Chapter 15

Victory at Last

May 6, 1778, was a day of celebration that George Washington and the men at Valley Forge would remember for the rest of their lives. It was the day they received word that France had officially joined them in the war against the British. Now the Americans would get something vital they had lacked up until now: a strong navy to break the British blockades of the rebel colonies.

Other news arrived at the same time. General Howe had been relieved of his command of the British forces, and General Henry Clinton had replaced him.

Within days there was still more news. Spies informed George that the British were planning to evacuate Philadelphia and head back to New York. The British were moving their forces because when the French fleet arrived, it could easily sail up the Delaware River and attack the British troops stationed in the city. Now George and his men had something to do! The patriots marched out of Valley Forge to cut off the British en route to New York.

On June 28, in record-breaking heat, the troops met near the courthouse in Monmouth, New Jersey. It was another bloody battle, and George was shocked to find that one of his generals, Charles Lee, had panicked and ordered his men back from the battle lines. George whipped his horse into action and ordered the men back into attack positions. A year or so earlier many of the men would have deserted at such an order, but Baron von Steuben's training paid off. The men obeyed their commander and regrouped into ranks. George himself led them toward the redcoats, musket balls falling all around him. When his horse dropped dead from exhaustion, he called for another one, climbed on, and led another charge.

As night fell, the British escaped from the battlefield and headed for nearby Sandy Hook, where Royal Navy ships were waiting to take them to New York. Although the British got away, they paid a heavy price in dead and wounded in the attack, while only seventy-two Continental soldiers were killed. George was satisfied with the result. Thanks to Baron von Steuben, patriot soldiers were now efficient, well-trained fighters—fighters who he hoped would soon win the war.

Twelve days later seventeen French warships were anchored off Sandy Hook. George hoped their commander would agree to a combined land and sea attack on New York. However, the French commander would not brave the cannons that defended New York. Instead the ships sailed north to reclaim Newport, Rhode Island, from the British. On the way there, heavy storms blew up along the eastern seaboard, and the French fleet turned around and sailed off to calmer waters in their colonies in the West Indies.

Both George and General Lafayette were so disappointed by the French navy's actions that they could hardly bear to discuss it. Lafayette decided to return home to France for a visit. His purpose was twofold. He wanted to see his new son, who had been named George Washington Lafayette, and he hoped to talk King Louis XVI into sending more military help.

George hoped his young friend would be able to do just that, since the British were on the move again. This time they were headed south, and spies reported they believed many loyalists there would fight alongside them. This prospect alarmed George greatly because the southern colonies produced a lot of the items necessary for war. They grew the tobacco and rice that were traded with France and Holland for gunpowder and cannons, and the best war horses were bred there.

The British, though, were determined, and by New Year's Day 1779 the city of Savannah and the Georgia colony were back in British hands. Their next target was Charleston, South Carolina, where, after a six-week siege, General Benjamin Lincoln surrendered to the British.

Without the French navy to oppose them, British troops were transported by ship up and down the coastline, and there was little George could do to stop them.

Meanwhile the Continental Congress sent General Horatio Gates off to command the southern army. George was not happy about this decision. He did not trust Gates and felt that as commander in chief he should have been consulted ahead of time about the decision.

George was even more upset when his feelings about Gates proved accurate. In a battle near Camden, South Carolina, on August 16, Gates's troops clashed with those of General Cornwallis. When the redcoats appeared to have the upper hand, Gates turned his horse from the battle and galloped away at top speed. He had covered sixty miles before he stopped, leaving his men to slug it out with the British alone. Over a thousand of the men died in the battle. George was bitter toward the Congress for giving Gates more military power than he had proved himself ready to handle. The Congress quickly reversed itself and relieved Gates of his command. This time it asked George to recommend his best officer for the job. Without hesitation, George chose Nathanael Greene.

In April Lafayette returned with good news! The king of France was sending more ships along with troops. Soon five thousand French soldiers arrived.

Two months later George and Count de Rochambeau, the French military leader, had a two-day meeting in Hartford, Connecticut. Lafayette, who now spoke good English, joined them as an interpreter. George walked into the first meeting optimistic that the war would soon be over. With the help of the French troops the patriots could march on New York and oust the British. They could then move south, sweeping the redcoats off the North American continent before them.

By the end of the meeting, however, George was a deflated man. Yes, Count de Rochambeau agreed with George that it would be possible to beat the British in New York if they joined forces, but he did not want to. Not, at least, until the French navy arrived with ships to back them up from the sea. George tried to hide his frustration and disappointment. After all, if he pushed his view too hard, the French might leave, and that would be a disaster.

To clear his head after the meeting, George rode on to West Point to inspect the fortress and visit with his friend General Benedict Arnold, whom he had recently appointed as commander there. George was eager to see all of the improvements at West Point that Congress had sent money for.

On September 25, 1780, George, along with Generals Knox and Lafayette and a 160-man escort, arrived at Beverly, across the Hudson River from West Point. As George crossed the river on a ferry, he was surprised not to hear a cannon salute. After all, Benedict Arnold knew he was coming. However, when he reached the other side, George forgot about the salute. He was too shocked by the state of the fort to give it another thought.

It was unbelievable. Benedict Arnold had written in such glowing terms about all the expensive improvements he had made, but George's eyes told him a different story. The barracks were falling down, the walls had gaping holes in them, and the cannons were not even in firing position! Two hours later, George was still stunned at the shambles West Point was in, and Benedict Arnold had not shown his face.

Eventually, George decided he would have to find him. He crossed the river back to Beverly, where Benedict Arnold and his beautiful young wife lived. George and his generals were welcomed inside Arnold's house by the butler, who showed them to the dining room, where a sumptuous lunch was laid out. But there was still no sign of either the host or hostess.

As George removed his hat and gloves, he soon found out why. An aide handed him a thick package that had just arrived. George broke open the seal and pulled out a wad of documents. As he began to read the first one, his hands started to shake. A letter from a Colonel Jameson stationed near New York said that John André had been caught in civilian clothes trying to make his way into the city. Stuffed in his boots were all the papers now in the envelope. As George leafed through them, he saw letters from John André to Benedict Arnold and vice versa. There were also detailed plans of West Point and the surrounding area, and even a log of where George and his officers would be at any time during the visit to West Point.

George could draw only one conclusion from the documents, but it was almost too horrible to contemplate. Since John André was commander of the British spy network, Benedict Arnold was a traitor!

"Quickly," George said to his aide, "take a man with you and go in search of General Arnold. He may be crossing the river. If you find him, detain him and bring him to me."

"Yes, sir," the aide replied with a puzzled look.

When the aide had left, George slumped into a nearby chair. He put his head in his hands and wept. "Arnold has betrayed me. Who can I trust now?" he whispered to himself.

Later that day George was furious to learn that the same officer who had sent the papers to him, unaware that they incriminated Benedict Arnold, had sent a letter to Arnold telling him about John André's capture. Inadvertently tipped off, Benedict Arnold had just enough time to escape to a British ship.

John André was tried for being a spy and sentenced to death by hanging. George tried vainly to get the British to swap him for Benedict Arnold, whom he felt deserved the punishment much more, but the British would not agree to a deal, and so John André was hanged. Meanwhile Benedict Arnold was given a prominent position in the British army and became one of the Americans' most knowledgeable and hated opponents.

It took George a long time to recover from the shock of learning that Benedict Arnold was a traitor. Not only had Arnold been willing to sell secrets that would allow the British to overrun West Point, but he had also given over information that would have made it possible for the English to capture George and the generals with him.

As another awful winter passed, the Continental army once again camped at Morristown, New Jersey. By spring 1781 George Washington was ready for some sign of hope. It came in the form of a letter from Count de Rochambeau promising that his army would be ready to join George's north of New York in July. Earlier in the year spies had told George that British General Clinton was worried about a combined American and French attack. As a result he had ordered General Cornwallis, who was ravaging North Carolina and Virginia, to pull back in case reinforcements were needed for the battle in New York. And that is what General Cornwallis did. He pulled his troops back to the York peninsula in Virginia.

George Washington and Count de Rochambeau seized on this opportunity. If they marched their armies to Virginia, they, with the help of the French navy, could trap General Cornwallis and deal the British a crushing blow. In August the two armies began the long march from New York to Virginia. They left a skeleton army behind to fool General Clinton into thinking they still intended to attack New York. If the British commander got wind that they really intended to attack General Cornwallis, he would most certainly send reinforcements to strengthen the redcoats in Virginia.

On September 5, soon after George Washington's army had marched through Philadelphia, a message arrived for him. It was a letter from the French Admiral Count de Grasse. His fleet of warships had finally reached the entrance to Chesapeake Bay. Everything was falling into place.

While the men marched south, George decided to ride on ahead and visit Mount Vernon. Two men accompanied him, his black servant Billy Lee and an aide. George did not fear being caught by the British. He was on his home territory now. Not only did he know every road in the area, he was still one of the fastest horsemen in all Virginia—just let anyone try to catch him!

The three men spent the first night in Baltimore and then galloped on to Mount Vernon. As George rode up the tree-lined driveway, he could scarcely believe it. It had been six and a half years since he had last seen his beloved plantation. Martha and his four grandchildren waited on the veranda as George dismounted with the agility of a man half his age. George greeted Martha warmly and swept the little grandson he had never seen into his arms. The boy was named George Washington Parke Custis, and George thought him adorable. George did not mind it one bit that his three granddaughters also clambered over their grandfather.

George stayed at Mount Vernon for several days, making war plans and eating enough food to make up for all the meals he had missed on the trip south. When he left the plantation, one more rider accompanied him—his stepson, Jacky, a man who had spent the seven years of the Revolutionary War avoiding the fighting. Now that George told him there was a real chance the Americans and the French might be able to defeat General Cornwallis, Jacky was gripped with a longing to see some action. Not that he wanted to be involved in the fighting. He told his stepfather that he would like to be seated in a coach at the rear, with a good view of what was going on. George agreed to take him along, though he did not care for Jacky's attitude.

On September 18 George was reunited with his army at Williamsburg. From there he and Count de Rochambeau went to meet French Admiral Count de Grasse on his ship, the *Ville de Paris*. When George had scrambled aboard, the six-foot-two admiral greeted him in a typical French manner. "My dear little general!" he exclaimed as he kissed George on both cheeks. George's aides laughed so hard they cried.

In spite of its beginning, the meeting was very serious. The three commanders agreed that the British army should be cut off at Yorktown and kept under siege until it surrendered. This plan made Count de Rochambeau very happy, since he was one of Europe's best "siegemasters." With twenty-one thousand French and American troops and the admiral's fleet blocking the British escape by sea, it seemed they had General Cornwallis at last.

Even though George was nervous that something unforeseen would interrupt their plans, everything went like clockwork. Count de Rochambeau set to work organizing the men. On October 9 George lit the fuse of the first cannon to be fired at the siege on Yorktown while his stepson, Jacky, sat in a carriage watching from a safe distance.

Heavy shelling continued day after day. The British fought on, but there was no way they could win, since they would eventually run out of food and supplies. At one stage they attempted to run away across the York River, but a storm blew up, making it too rough for them to launch their boats. Finally, after eight days, the moment George had dreamed about for years occurred. A British drummer began beating a different tune—the tune of surrender. Then an officer waving a white flag walked from his line toward the Americans. The bombing stopped, and the officer delivered his message. General Cornwallis was ready to surrender!

Chapter 16

Peace at Last

George Washington adjusted the feather on his hat and straightened his lapels. It was ten minutes to three on October 19, 1781, and he had an important task ahead of him. He strolled out of the tent and mounted his horse with the aid of his servant. As he trotted his horse out of camp, George saw two lines of soldiers stretching a mile and a half from the Continental army camp to Yorktown. The French were on his right and Americans on his left.

At the far end of the road, at the stroke of three o'clock, the first regiment of British soldiers marched toward George. George gave the order for the American band to strike up. He had selected the tune to which the British were to march to their surrender. It was a children's nursery song called "The World Turned Upside Down." The words ran through George's mind as he watched regiment after regiment stream out of Yorktown and form into ranks.

> If ponies rode men and the grass ate cows;
> And cats should be chased into holes by the
>   mouse;
> If the mammas sold their babies to the
>   gypsies for half a crown;
> If summer were spring and the other way
>   round;
> Then all the world would be upside down.

It was a fitting tune because this was unlike any other moment George had experienced. He was watching the world turned upside down. Within a few minutes British General Cornwallis was going to formally surrender over 7,250 soldiers, 850 sailors, 244 cannons, and all of their firearms to the ragtag American army. One quarter of Great Britain's fighting troops in North America were about to be placed under George Washington's control.

As the redcoats approached George and his generals, their drums and fifes were draped in black, and their battle flags were furled. Many of the soldiers wept openly as they laid down their muskets and turned toward the French army. Regiments of Hessian soldiers followed. But unlike the British, they looked relieved it was all over.

Minutes later General Charles O'Hara stepped forward holding a sword in both his hands. George was surprised because in the surrender talks it had been agreed that General Cornwallis would be the one to formally surrender to the Americans.

"General Cornwallis is sick," General O'Hara said. "He has asked me to represent him in the surrender ceremony."

Sick, George thought to himself. *He's sick all right, sick at the thought of giving his sword to a rebel!*

"Very well," George said. "Continue."

The music stopped, and everything was silent as General O'Hara turned away from George and offered the sword to General Rochambeau, a French officer.

George wasn't surprised. He'd noticed that the British men would not look at the Americans. It was too much for their pride to bear. It was one thing to be beaten by a world power like the French, but quite another to be whipped by thirteen of their wayward colonies.

The French general shook his head and pointed to George. "No," he said. "We serve under the Americans. General Washington will give you orders."

George suddenly remembered how the British had humiliated General Benjamin Lincoln and his troops when the patriots surrendered in Charleston. An idea came to him. "I will not accept it either," George told him. "I want you to surrender the sword to General Lincoln. He will be my representative."

Everyone watched as General O'Hara hesitated, tears streaming down his cheeks. Then General O'Hara held out Cornwallis's sword to General

Lincoln. The band struck up "Yankee Doodle Dandy," and the patriots grinned.

Although the war was not officially over, George hoped that General Cornwallis's surrender would send a message to King George and Parliament that it was pointless to go on.

Once the surrender ceremony was over, many practical matters had to be attended to. George took great care to make sure that everything was done according to the rules of warfare. All surrendering officers were given the opportunity to sign a paper stating that they would never again fight in America and that if they broke their vow and were caught, they would be executed. Regular soldiers were marched off to prison camps until negotiators from both sides could work out arrangements on how to get them home. George also ordered a victory dispatch be written and sent to Congress, informing them of the day's events. Then, as a matter of courtesy, George sat down to dine with General Charles O'Hara.

Even as George was enjoying the sight of British ships sailing away from the colonies, his mind was on the leave he was planning to take. He was exhausted from so many years of war, and he had decided to spend a quiet week with his wife and Jacky's growing family before returning to the battlefront. George was particularly looking forward to spending some more time with his new grandson.

George planned to stop in at Martha's sister's house at Eltham, Virginia. Jacky was staying there, recovering from a sore throat and aching muscles, symptoms that had developed the same day the surrender ceremony took place. George hoped he was feeling much better by now so that they could continue on to Mount Vernon together.

George left for Eltham early on the morning of November 4, 1781. At every village along the way he was greeted with bonfires, bands, and patriotic songs, many of which mentioned the "gallant General Washington." He was told that citizens even sang them as hymns in church. George blushed every time he heard one of these songs!

When he reached Martha's sister's house late in the evening, George was shocked to learn that Jacky was seriously ill with camp fever. Indeed, Martha had come from Mount Vernon, and she joined Jacky's wife, Nelly, and their oldest daughter, five-year-old Eliza, in keeping watch at his bedside.

George had seen camp fever hundreds of times before, and although he tried to offer words of hope to Martha and Nelly, his heart was not in it. He felt sure that twenty-eight-year-old Jacky was dying, and so he was. By the next morning George was arranging his stepson's funeral service.

Martha, Nelly, and Eliza were distraught over Jacky's death. Jacky was Martha's last child, and she sobbed bitterly for days. George thought it was ironic. Jacky, the man who would not fight, had caught a deadly virus while watching a battle from a safe distance.

Finally George returned to Mount Vernon, but it was a house of mourning, and he was anxious to leave again.

On November 20 George left for Philadelphia. He was glad he had been able to convince Martha to come with him. He had been worried that she would become sick with grief if she were left behind.

As George left Mount Vernon, one matter weighed heavy on his mind: the problem of prisoners of war. The Americans held over ten thousand British and Hessian soldiers, including about fifty-seven hundred who had surrendered at Saratoga nearly five years before. It took many American soldiers to guard all of these prisoners and a lot of money to feed them. George knew that the British had not looked after their colonial prisoners so well. Instead of keeping most of them on land, they had loaded them onto ships and kept them in the British-controlled harbors. No one was ever able to give George an accurate count of all the prisoners who had died on board these ships, but it was estimated that about ten thousand colonial soldiers had already died on prison ships in New York and Charleston harbors.

By Christmas wonderful news had arrived. Lord North, the prime minister of Great Britain, had finally had enough of the war. In fact, the war had brought about the exact opposite of what it was supposed to achieve. Taxes in Britain were now higher than ever, the lives of many thousands of British soldiers had been lost, and it was nearly impossible to raise any more volunteers. The people of Britain had grown weary of the war. However, George heard that King George III had a difficult time accepting the idea of surrender. King George pouted and offered to resign as king, but when no one begged him to stay, he changed his mind and accepted what Parliament was telling him. The time had come for peace.

In March 1782 the Continental Congress sent Benjamin Franklin, John Adams, John Jay, and Henry Laurens to France to work out a peace treaty with England's new prime minister, Lord Rockingham.

Meanwhile George, accompanied by Martha, returned with his Continental troops to their camp at Newburgh, New York. Until the war was officially over, anything could happen, including more fighting. However, it was no surprise to George when the next battle he faced was not between the loyalists and the patriots but between army men and the Congress. It was every bit as serious as the battles he had faced over the past six years, perhaps more so because it threatened everything George had fought for.

The battle was over money. The Continental Congress had not paid the regular soldiers for months and was refusing to say where it would get the money needed to pay all of their back pay and benefits. The Congress found itself without enough money to fulfill its promises because it did not have the power to raise taxes. Only the individual colonies had the power to tax their own citizens. The Congress asked the colonies to send money to pay the soldiers, but since the war was nearly over, none of them wanted to spend any more money.

Each colony thought the other colonies should pay up first. As a result none of them paid.

It was not long before groups of soldiers were talking about taking over the newly freed colonies and establishing one strong government with a king as head who could tax everyone. One group, led by Colonel Lewis Nicola, even had a plan for who should rule this new monarchy. It was none other than George Washington.

In May 1782 George opened a letter marked "confidential" from Colonel Nicola. As he read it, a sickening feeling gripped his stomach. Lewis Nicola wrote that he and many other army officers were willing to help George seize power and become the new king of America!

George was appalled by what he read. He had not fought a war to make himself a king or a dictator. He wrote back to Colonel Nicola and told him that he was dedicated to a democratic republic. Americans did not need another King George. What they needed was a strong government where the people had a say over their own destiny. After all, it was the fact that the colonists did not have the same rights as Englishmen that had begun the revolution in the first place. They needed to take the good parts of the British system of government but leave out the king!

The idea of a king slowly died down as the peace treaty talks dragged on. It was November before the first draft of a treaty was completed. In this Treaty of Paris, as it was called, the British guaranteed America's independence and agreed to new borders for the new nation. America would stretch west from the Atlantic coast to the Mississippi River, and south from the Great Lakes to the boundary of Florida, which belonged to the Spanish.

Since things had progressed this far, everyone agreed that peace was just around the corner. The British fleet withdrew from Charleston in early December, and the French army responded by gathering up all of its equipment and sailing for home early in the new year, 1783. It was very difficult for George to say good-bye to his old friend General Lafayette, who had become like a son to him.

After the French withdrawal George Washington's battles continued. Rumors started to circulate that the Continental Congress was not going to honor its promises now that the war was at an end. According to an unsigned letter called the "Newburgh Address," there would be no back pay for the army, no pensions for the families of dead soldiers, and no aid for disabled veterans.

Tempers grew white hot. Whole regiments threatened to march to the western frontier and set up a new state there, leaving the thirteen colonies unprotected. Others talked of storming the Congress and taking by force the money they were owed.

All of this put George in an awkward position. He had sympathies for both sides in the argument. On the one hand he agreed with the men. It was only fair that they should get the money they had earned with their blood and sweat. On the other hand, George knew every man in the Congress, and he was sure that when they said they did not have the money, they were telling the truth. The problem lay with the lack of organized government, not with the individual delegates to the Congress.

On March 15, 1783, the situation became so tense that George feared a blood bath. He knew he had to do something. After much thought he called a meeting of all his officers at the Temple, a cavernous wooden building that doubled as both a dance hall and a church.

George looked sadly out over the men who had served with such bravery. Many of them were as close to him as his own brothers. Now no one spoke. The men sat stony-faced, arms crossed, hardly seeming to care what their commander had to say. The time for talking was long past. Still, George cleared his throat and began to read from a speech he had prepared. "Let me entreat you, gentlemen, on your part not to take any measures which, viewed in the calm light of reason, will lessen the dignity and sully the glory you have hitherto maintained..."

As he looked anxiously over the crowd, George could sense that no one was moved by his speech. He stopped reading, folded the paper, and put it in his pocket. Then he quietly took out a letter from a member of Congress promising to find the money somewhere. The writing on this document was much smaller, and George did something he had never done before in public. He pulled out his reading glasses. "Gentlemen," he said as he placed them on his face, "you will permit me to put on my spectacles, for I have not only grown gray but almost blind in the service of my country." After reading the letter, George spoke from his heart. He urged the men to be patient and reminded them that they had fought so hard for a free country and should not consider abandoning it now that peace was at hand.

Much to George's relief, the men began to listen to him, and by the time the meeting was over, they had committed to staying in uniform and asked him to become their spokesman before Congress.

In the course of the meeting George Washington had done something just as important as winning any battle. He had saved the country from the predictable result of revolution—lawlessness and more bloodshed.

Few people understood what George had done, but that didn't worry him. As far as he was concerned, the fewer people who knew about the situation the better.

As the weeks went by, George gave a lot of thought to what should happen when the war was officially over. He was sure the only way for the American colonies to survive was for them to band together as a group who would agree to protect one another and work together in peace. If this did not happen, he was concerned that America would become the laughingstock of Europe and eventually the colonists would need the British to come back and once again rule over them. To make sure this did not happen, George wrote a circular explaining what he thought should happen when peace was finally declared. He began by apologizing for "stepping out of the proper line of duty," since he was a military man and not a politician. Then he wrote:

> There are four things which I humbly conceive are essential to the well-being, I may even venture to say, to the existence of the United States as an independent power:
>
> 1st. An indissoluble Union of the States under one Federal Head.
>
> 2ndly. A sacred regard for public justice.
>
> 3rdly. The adoption of a proper peace establishment, and
>
> 4thly. The prevalence of that pacific and friendly disposition among the people of the United States which will induce them to forget their local prejudices and policies, to make those mutual concessions which are requisite to the general prosperity, and in some instances, to sacrifice their individual advantages to the interest of the community.

On November 1 a ship brought word to George Washington that the final peace treaty between Britain and its former colonies had been signed two months earlier on September 3, 1783. The war was truly over! The only job that remained was to supervise the British withdrawal of their remaining troops from American soil. The treaty also suggested that the patriots return loyalists' property to them and treat them with kindness. New York had been held by the British since 1776, and during that time thousands of colonists loyal to King George had fled there for safety. These people were now angry that the king had abandoned them to the very patriots they had partnered with the British to defeat.

Most patriots were willing to deal fairly with the British and Hessian soldiers, but their blood ran cold when they thought of what the loyalists had done to their fellow Americans. Even small children sang rhymes about what should happen to the loyalists in New York. "Tories, with their brats and wives, should fly to save their wretched lives."

As George marched his army toward New York City one last time, twenty-five thousand loyalists clambered aboard ships bound for England, Canada, and the West Indies. Nearly three times as many had already left American shores earlier in the revolution. Among them were Benedict Arnold and Benjamin Franklin's son, William. William Franklin had been the pro-British governor of New Jersey and had made himself even more unpopular by heading up the Board of Associated Loyalists and ordering the revenge killing of patriot soldiers who were supposed to be under his protection.

The Continental army arrived in New York City on November 26, 1783. Nine days later the last British ship sailed out of the harbor.

Now that the war was truly over, George Washington had one more thing to do, something he dreaded. He had to say good-bye to his officers.

At noon on December 4 a group of twenty long-faced men sat around a large table at Fraunces Tavern on Pearl Street. Plenty of food and wine had been left behind by the British, but no one was in a festive mood. George barely touched his plate, nor did the men around him. Now their victory was mixed with the sorrow of parting. George's heart thumped when he realized it was time for him to stand and give one last toast. "With a heart full of love and gratitude, I now take leave of you. I most devoutly wish that your later days may be as prosperous and happy as your former ones have been glorious and honorable," he said, his voice thick with emotion. "I cannot come to each of you, but shall feel obliged if each of you will come and take my hand."

There was a long silence. Then Henry Knox, the artillery expert, pushed back his chair and walked up to George. As he reached out to shake his commander's hand, it was more than George could bear. He threw his arms open, embraced Henry, and kissed him on the cheek. All around the room men pulled out handkerchiefs or wiped their eyes with the back of their hands. George handed Henry his discharge papers and an IOU issued by Congress for his back pay. Silently the men stepped forward one by one to embrace their commander in chief and receive their discharge papers. By the end of the proceedings there was not a dry eye in the tavern.

When every man had stepped forward, George signaled to his aide and walked out of the room. He stopped at the doorway, turned, and waved his hat at the men. Then he was gone.

Outside the tavern Martha was waiting for him in a carriage. George sat silently, lost in his own thoughts. Outside the crowds cheered exuberantly as the carriage passed by. The Washingtons boarded a barge that conveyed them over the Hudson River to New Jersey to begin the trip back to Virginia.

On December 23 George rode into Annapolis, Maryland, to stand before Congress one last time. With trembling hands he drew the papers commissioning him as commander of the Continental army from his breast pocket and handed them back to the president of the Continental Congress, Thomas Mifflin. Eight years before, Thomas Mifflin had been one of the two aides who set out for Boston with George to take command of the Continental army.

George read a speech to the hushed crowd.

> Mr. President...I now have the honor of offering my sincere Congratulations to Congress and of presenting myself before them to surrender into their hands the trust committed to me, and to claim the indulgence of retiring from the service of my country.

George choked back tears as he continued.

> Having now finished the work assigned me, I retire from the great theatre of action; and bidding an Affectionate farewell to this

August body under whose orders I have so
long acted, I here offer my commission, and
take my leave of all the employments of
public life.

Chapter 17

A Rising Sun

George and Martha Washington sat side by side in their carriage on Christmas Eve, 1783. "Just think of it, Martha!" George exclaimed. "For the first time in thirty years, I'm a private citizen. No more politics or war for me." Then he drew back the curtain over the window. Outside he caught his first glimpse of his beloved Mount Vernon covered in a thick blanket of snow. "Oh, how wonderful it is to be home at last." After eight years of constantly moving around, George could hardly believe he was really going to return to the life of a planter.

Waiting at the door for them were Nelly and her four small children. They had all been staying at Mount Vernon since Jacky's death.

"How wonderful to see you again," George said, lifting two-year-old George Washington Custis (whom everyone now called Wash) into the air.

Wash looked shyly at George.

"He hardly remembers you," Martha said. "We have a lot of reacquainting to do, don't we, children?"

As it happened, George had plenty of opportunity over the next two months to get to know the children better. A blizzard hit the area, and he could not get out to inspect the plantation until the end of February.

Still, George kept busy. On the day after Christmas he spread piles of papers out on the desk in his office. As he did so, his cousin, Lund Washington, knocked on the door and came in.

"I'm glad you're here!" George said. "I've spent the past two hours trying to sort out the latest deed claims to my land holdings. I don't think I've made any progress at all."

Lund looked painfully embarrassed. "Urr, umm," he replied, "certain things have not been easy to keep up during the war. I'm afraid your paperwork has suffered greatly. I am not naturally inclined to figures, though I was able to keep it in order until the British came up the river."

"And?" George asked, staring gloomily at the piles of paper.

"Well," Lund went on, "I threw all the important papers into a trunk and fled with them. I knew you would want them saved if they attacked. Unfortunately, after four or five evacuations I lost all sense of order to them. I must apologize."

George groaned. It would take several days to sort the mess out, but he would have to. As well as finding the deeds, he needed to find some papers relating to Jacky's will. And then there was Patsy's estate, which had not yet been properly settled. The war had interrupted letters to England, and George needed to follow up on the money he was owed for some shares that Patsy had owned in England.

Lund interrupted George's thoughts. "There's another matter, too. One that I hesitated to bring up when you were last home. I didn't want to disturb you, but now it has to be addressed."

George walked over to the fire and warmed his hands. "I'll order coffee for us," he said. "Go on."

This time Lund looked even more awkward. "It's about my pay. In the time you have been away, so many of your renters have not been able to make much money off their plots. The currency kept devaluing, and many of the men were away fighting. I haven't been able to collect the rent from them for five years, and so I have not drawn my own salary."

"Well, you will have to give me a little time while I get this in order," George said, waving a hand in the direction of his desk. "But you will get your money. Is there anything else of importance I should know?"

During the next two hours George and Lund discussed other matters that George had known about but had not had time to attend to. As best they could work out, George and Martha still owned about two hundred slaves, though eighteen of them had taken advantage of a British raid on the crops at Mount Vernon and run away. It was a common enough problem in the southern colonies.

Over twenty-five thousand slaves had run away. Lund explained that wanted posters had been made up and posses sent out after them, but the slaves had not been caught. Nine more slaves had been sold during the war to pay taxes.

There was also bad new about Belvoir, the Fairfax mansion that held so many wonderful memories for George. Just weeks before Christmas it was burned to the ground. Although no one was sure what caused the blaze, Lund thought it had probably been struck by lightning. George knew the fire made it even more unlikely that he would ever see George and Sally Fairfax again. He decided to write to them the following morning and tell them the bad news.

George had many other letters to write, as mail started arriving at Mount Vernon by the sackful. This cost George money that he did not have on hand. Postage due on a letter was paid by the person receiving it. It didn't cost Americans anything to write to their hero in Virginia, so thousands of people wrote. Some letters asked George to run for public office again. Others wanted money from him, or even his signature. Many people wanted his picture, and soon portrait artists were arriving at George's door asking him to pose for them.

Most of the time George obliged. He did not like sitting still, but he was a patient man. He even allowed the famous French sculptor Jean Antoine Houdon to cover his face in clay to make a mask. The mask was used to produce a clay bust of George that Congress had commissioned. George

was relieved it was only a bust Houdon was producing, as he wouldn't have to wear the toga the
sculptor normally draped his famous subjects in.

When George's six-year-old step-granddaughter
saw George lying on a table with a white sheet over
him to keep the clay off his clothes, she ran away
screaming, "Popa's dead." She would not be
silenced until Houdon lifted the sheet and George
waved his fingers at her.

Before long George Washington was the most
recognized person in America. And when people
saw his portrait or read a letter he had sent them,
the next thing they wanted to do was visit him.
And so they did. Southern manners dictated that if
a person, even an uninvited stranger, came to your
house at mealtime, he or she was to be fed, and if
that visitor was still there at bedtime, he or she
should be invited to stay overnight.

When spring arrived people came every day to
visit and sleep over. On most evenings the
Washingtons sat down to dinner with at least eight
or ten visitors, as well as Lund Washington, Nelly,
and her four children. Sometimes George felt as
though he was running an inn—with one difference. No one paid for his or her lodging. The food
and wine flowed freely, and George paid for it all.
Even when he did not have much spare cash, he
always took great pride in setting a "plentiful" table
for his guests, whoever they were.

George enjoyed most of all spending evenings
with old friends. Sometimes he and Dr. Craik would
sit on the veranda and reminisce about times like

General Braddock's ghastly defeat and the Seven Years' War. Other times, George would ask the doctor his advice about the rheumatism that was starting to bother him, and especially about his teeth, which were a nightmare. During the war several of his teeth had been pulled, but Dr. Craik told George the rest would have to go as well. This set George on the trail of the best false teeth available. The best he could buy were carved from elephant tusks and wired onto a metal jaw with a hinge at the back. The whole contraption was incredibly heavy, and George hated wearing it. The only thing he hated more was to be seen without any teeth at all.

Besides constantly searching for more comfortable false teeth, George kept busy and happy supervising his plantation, which had not been run efficiently while he was gone.

Martha was happy, too. Nelly Custis remarried, but her children had grown so attached to George and Martha that she asked them to adopt her two youngest children, Nelly and Wash. Once again George had two young children to take care of, along with the many other children who came to stay with him at Mount Vernon. Fielding Lewis, his sister Betty's husband, had recently died, leaving her with six children, and they often came to stay. As well, George's younger brother Sam had died of tuberculosis near the end of the war. He'd had five wives, most of whom had died in childbirth. Among them they had produced eleven children, five of whom were still alive. They, too, came for long visits with Uncle George and Aunt Martha. And since Sam had died in debt, George paid for his children to go to school. Eventually Sam's nine-year-old daughter Harriet moved in permanently, as did Fanny Bassett, the teenage daughter of Martha's deceased sister.

In the quietness of his office George continued to read the newspaper. Many of his old friends from Congress kept in touch with him, though he was sure he would never return to public life. However, matters were not going well for the new nation. There were many things it did not have. One of them was a name, but other matters were more important than that. When the colonies were part of the British Empire, the empire protected them and gave them laws and a system of government. Now they were supposed to do all of this for themselves, and it was proving nearly impossible.

The problem was that the individual states (formerly the colonies) did not want to work together. States taxed one another for every pound of flour or pair of shoes that were sold across a state's border. North African pirates plundered American ships on the high seas, and Britain, realizing that no one could do anything about it, was refusing to leave the western forts it had agreed to leave in the Treaty of Paris. And many Indians were still loyal to the British and refused to accept America as a nation. Also, in the Treaty of Paris Britain had agreed to hand over the western land it had taken from the French in the Seven Years' War. It had indeed kept its word, and now there was constant bickering over which state got which piece of "new" land. Big states like Virginia thought they deserved a lot of this land, and the smaller states fretted over the larger states getting even larger.

In the far west, Spain, which claimed Louisiana, refused to allow Americans to ship their trading goods down the Mississippi River to the port of New Orleans. As a result western farmers had no way to get their produce to market.

All of this worried George. While leading the army, he had worked with men from every state and had visited many parts of the country. He saw America as one country, with one common set of needs, not as thirteen small countries, each trying to make it on its own.

While the country struggled on, George continued planting trees on his property and breeding jackasses. He hoped things would improve for America. But in March 1786 he received a letter from Henry Knox telling him about Shays's Rebellion. As he read the letter, he knew his hopes would not be realized. George could understand why the rebellion had taken place. Farmers in western Massachusetts were furious over their high taxes. Many of them were faced with selling their land to pay them. A man named Daniel Shays led twelve hundred farmers, pitchforks in hand, in a violent protest. The farmers shut down the courts, emptied the debtors' prisons, and disrupted land auctions. Eventually four thousand militiamen were sent in to calm things down. Four protesters were killed in the bloody conflict.

Although George could understand the farmers' frustration, he was appalled by their actions, and more so because Daniel Shays was a patriot who had fought in the battles of Lexington, Bunker Hill, and Saratoga. But all over America trained fighting men were frustrated with the way things were turning out. Unless something changed fast, George was sure that Shays's Rebellion would be the first in a long string of conflicts between the people and their new government. What was happening was the exact opposite of what he had given eight years of his life to fight for!

By April 1787 George knew he would have to leave his peaceful home on the Potomac, at least for a short while. He had received many letters and personal visits from members of the Continental Congress urging him to get involved in politics again and become part of the next Congress. George was smart enough to know why people like Benjamin Franklin, James Madison, and Alexander Hamilton wanted him there. The Articles of Confederation were not working. George referred to them as a "rope of sand." And while the Congress legally could only amend them, George was certain this next Congress would try to scrap them altogether and work out a whole new form of government. George was by far the most popular and trusted man in America, and if he was there, many people would be willing to go along with any changes that were made.

This was fine with George. He wanted change as much as anyone, and so he was happy to be sent as a delegate from Virginia to the convention to revise the Articles of Confederation.

On May 9, 1787, George stopped in to visit his sick mother and then rode on to Philadelphia, the site of the convention, where he arrived on May 13. Word had already reached the people of Philadelphia that he was coming. Crowds lined the streets to catch a glimpse of their "American Hero," and the Liberty Bell tolled, just as it had over ten years before when the Declaration of Independence was signed.

Only one other delegate was on time for the convention, and it wasn't until twelve days later that twenty-nine delegates from seven states showed up, enough to form a quorum. George was glad all fifty-five delegates were not there at the beginning, as the city was in the grip of a heat wave. The convention met in the Pennsylvania State House, and a layer of dirt had been spread over the cobblestones on the street outside to muffle the noise of carriage wheels. The dirt attracted thousands of flies, and although the windows in the State House were locked for secrecy, the flies managed to find their way inside. And as the temperature rose, so too did the smell. George, like most men of the time, bathed only once a week. So as sweat poured off the men as they met in the stifling confines of the State House, the pungent aroma of body odor filled the place.

The first matter of business was to elect a chairman for the discussions. Even though George had been out of circulation for some time, he was elected and took his place on stage. He sat on a high-backed wooden chair with a brown leather-upholstered cushion. A painted half-sun adorned the top of the chair back. It was a good thing the chair was comfortable because George sat in it all day, six days a week, for the next sixteen weeks while the delegates, who had shown up from every state except Rhode Island, argued about what an American government should be like.

Such a government had to be strong enough to protect the people and make America a powerful and respected country. But the government also had to have enough checks and balances so that the men in charge did not use their power to make themselves rich or act above the law.

Day after day the delegates argued, until a plan began to form. They thought it would be best to divide the government into three branches and make each branch separate from the others so that it couldn't tell the other two branches what to do. The first branch should be legislative. This branch would deal with making laws, and it would have the power to tax people, regulate trade in and out of the country, and issue money. Issuing money was very popular, since there were so many different types of currency in use in the former colonies.

The second branch of government would be judicial. The job of this branch was to make sure the laws were interpreted correctly and that people obeyed them. Citizens could ask for their case to be taken before a court, called the Supreme Court, if they felt they did not get justice from their own state court.

The third branch of government the delegates planned was the executive branch. This branch would be headed by a president appointed by an electoral college chosen by the state legislatures. The president would have control over the armed forces, conduct foreign policy, make federal appointments subject to the legislative branch's approval, and carry out the laws passed by the federal legislature. However, he would also have the power of veto over the legislative acts passed, which could be overturned only by a two-thirds vote of the legislators.

While some delegates thought a single president should head the executive branch, others argued that it would be better to have three presidents who had to agree before they made any decisions. Another question raised was how long the president or presidents should serve. Some delegates thought six years, while others thought a president should be appointed for life.

Other issues kept coming up. One of them was the problem of slavery. Since the war, many people, both black and white, thought it was strange that a nation whose rallying cry had been "Give me liberty or give me death" should have three quarters of a million people who were slaves. Indeed, five thousand slaves had fought in the War of Independence.

Many delegates, including Thomas Jefferson, fought hard to have slavery declared illegal in America. Others argued that slaves were property and that the federal government had no right to take a man's property away from him.

Eventually, after months of meetings, most delegates realized that no one was going to get everything he asked for. If they did not compromise, there would not be a United States and each of the former colonies would turn into separate little countries competing with each other. One of the compromises was over slavery. The practice was kept legal in the southern states, though the convention decided that new slaves could be imported from Africa for only twenty more years. After that the only new slaves would be those born on American soil. The delegates also agreed that the states that did not approve of slavery would have to return escaped slaves to their masters. As well, as America expanded to the west, there would be no slavery in the territory north of the Ohio River.

As the summer heat began to give way to the crispness of fall, the convention finally came up with a final draft of the proposed new Constitution of the United States. The straightforward document began:

> We the People of the United States, in order to form a more perfect Union, establish Justice, insure domestic Tranquility, provide for the common defense, promote the general Welfare, and secure the Blessings of Liberty to ourselves and our Posterity, do ordain and establish this Constitution of the United States of America.

On Monday, September 17, 1787, the convention met one last time. The delegates voted to support the Constitution and take it back to their states for final ratification.

Just as George Washington stood to dismiss the gathering, eighty-one-year-old Benjamin Franklin asked to speak. With tears streaming down his face, he began, "Throughout the often tiring weeks we have sat in this room together, I have puzzled over the painting of the sun which adorns the back of the chair on which General Washington has sat. I wondered if it represented a rising or a setting sun. Now I believe I know the answer. I have the happiness to know that it is a rising and not a setting sun."

Chapter 18

Mr. President

Two weeks after the close of the Constitutional Convention, George Washington was back at Mount Vernon supervising the completion of a new roof for part of the house. He had chosen a copper dove for the weathervane that would be mounted at the highest point of the roof. The dove was a symbol of peace, which more than anything is what George longed for: peace in the country, peace to live out his last few years on his own plantation. Yet George knew this was unlikely. It seemed that in every corner of every state arguments were taking place over ratifying the new Constitution.

One group, who called themselves anti-federalists, accused the Congress of being a group of rich men who were trying to make themselves the "unofficial lords" of America. Anti-federalists said the Constitution would give such people too much power to make laws that would make them richer. They also didn't think the federal government should be given so much power over the states. The federalists retorted that without one strong government every state would be weak and easily overtaken by Spain or Britain, with whom most of the states shared a border. Other people were concerned about the rights of citizens within each state. After being under Britain's thumb for so long, no one wanted to give his or her personal rights up to a big government in a faraway place.

In the end, the same process that had made the Constitution possible in the first place came into play: compromise. States agreed to ratify the document provided that the first thing the new government promised to do was create a Bill of Rights that guaranteed the rights of individuals.

First Delaware, then Pennsylvania, New Jersey, and Georgia, ratified the Constitution. As the months dragged on, Connecticut, Massachusetts, Maryland, and South Carolina followed. The entire country waited for one more state to ratify, giving the necessary nine states needed to establish the new government. Would it be North Carolina, Virginia, New Hampshire, New York, or Rhode Island? Finally, on June 21, 1788, George received word that New Hampshire had ratified the Constitution. The federal government of the United States of America was now official.

Amidst the debate over ratifying the Constitution, which took ten long months, George had his own private battle. He had emerged from the Revolutionary War not as *an* American hero but as *the* American hero, and now people assumed he would become the first president of the United States. Even George's old friend Lafayette wrote to him from France saying, "In the name of America, of mankind at large, and of your own fame, I beseech you, my dear General, not to deny your acceptance of the office of President for the first years." He finished with a statement George had heard a thousand times before: "You only can settle that political machine."

George was torn. He could see that he had a better chance of pulling the new government together than anyone else except perhaps Benjamin Franklin, who was now too old to be considered for the task. But would George's best be enough? Was it possible for any president to steer a path through the problems of the rights of individual states over the need for a central government? George did not know, but in the end he knew he had to do whatever he could to make the government work. So when on April 14, 1789, Congress sent word that it had unanimously voted for him to be the new president, George accepted the position.

Neither George nor Martha was eager to leave Mount Vernon again. In fact, Martha did not want to have any part in the inevitable celebrations that would accompany George's trip to New York, where he would be sworn in as president. She decided to stay at home until things settled down. Then she would travel to New York with ten-year-old Nelly and eight-year-old Wash.

At noon on April 23, 1789, George Washington rode into Elizabeth Town, New Jersey, on his large white horse. A drumroll sounded and an honor guard sprang to attention. The crowd cheered and waved. George rode to Elizabeth Town Point, where he dismounted and walked down the red carpet that had been laid over the roughhewn planks that formed the town's dock. Some women threw flowers at his feet, while others reached out to touch him. At the end of the dock a barge bobbed up and down in the water of Newark Bay. Several men in military uniforms rushed forward to help George aboard. Once George was safely seated on the vessel, the boatswain sounded his shrill whistle and the thirteen oarsmen, one from each state, rowed the barge out into the bay, and they all began the fifteen-mile trip to New York City.

As George journeyed across Newark Bay and into Kill van Kull, a flotilla trailed the barge until there were so many boats he lost count of them all. On the small docks that lined both sides of the kill people gathered and cheered.

When the barge finally entered New York Bay, two sloops came alongside. On one sloop a choir of twenty-five men and women serenaded George with patriotic songs. On the other sloop was a glee club of twelve men who raised their voices in harmony singing, "Welcome, mighty Chief once more! Welcome to this grateful shore!"

Nearby the *Galveston,* a Spanish man-of-war, hoisted the flags of twenty nations. The crew climbed up into the rigging and cheered George as the ship fired a fifteen-gun salute in his honor. Soon other ships joined in with their cannons. The noise rumbled across the bay as the barge passed Bedloe's Island and headed for Manhattan.

Finally the barge moved alongside Murray's Wharf at the bottom of Wall Street. A huge roar went up as George stepped ashore. The city was filled to overflowing with people who had come to witness this historic day. After being greeted by Governor Clinton of New York and various city officials, George, accompanied by an honor guard, made his way up Broadway, New York's main thoroughfare, to Number 3 Cherry Street, the first official residence of the United States president.

As he wound his way through the streets, George did not wave to the well-wishers who crowded around him or hung out of windows or leaned over balconies to see him. Instead he acknowledged them with a nod or a polite touch of his hat. George's head swirled with competing emotions. On the one hand, George was amazed and deeply touched that so many people had turned out to welcome him. On the other hand, their enthusiasm scared him. The people might cheer now, but would they still be cheering when as president he was forced to take actions that were not popular?

Finally they reached the President's House on Cherry Street. Inside, after meeting with still more dignitaries, George finally sank into a chair and relaxed away from the noisy crowd.

A week later, at 9 A.M. on Thursday, April 30, 1789, every church bell in the city began to peal. It was a cool, clear day—perfect for an inauguration—as people made their way to various churches to pray for the nation and its new president.

While the people prayed, George prepared himself for his inauguration. His gray hair was freshly powdered and tied back, and his manservant dressed him in a plain brown broadcloth suit. The fabric for the suit had been woven in Massachusetts, and George hoped it would send the message to American industry that the young nation could make it on its own. He pulled on his finest white silk stockings and slid his feet into black shoes with silver buckles. Then he placed a close-cropped brown beaver tricorner hat on his head. Before he left the house he strapped on a ceremonial sword.

Outside a white carriage was waiting to carry George to the old city hall on the corner of Wall and Broad Streets. The building had been taken over by the government and renamed Federal Hall.

As George stepped out onto the balcony from inside Federal Hall, the crowd erupted with a cheer. Men tossed their hats into the air, and women waved handkerchiefs. George was surprised by the size of the crowd. People packed tightly together seemed to stretch for as far as he could see.

Finally Robert Livingston, chancellor of New York state, stepped forward to administer the oath of office. Placing his hand on the Bible, George began the oath: "I solemnly swear that I will faithfully execute the office of President of the United States and will, to the best of my ability, preserve, protect, and defend the Constitution of the United

States." Then George added something that wasn't a required part of the oath. "So help me God!" he exclaimed as he lifted the Bible and kissed it.

Turning to face the crowd, Robert Livingston called out, "Long live George Washington, President of the United States." The crowd roared back, "God bless our president."

George bowed to the crowd and acknowledged their cheers. After several minutes he left the balcony and walked inside to deliver his inaugural address to Congress. It was a short speech, lasting only six minutes, in which he asked God to help the American people find liberty and happiness under their new government.

That night candles burned in every window in New York to celebrate the inauguration of the new president, and taverns overflowed with happy well-wishers. A two-hour fireworks display exploded above the city, drawing people, including the new president, out to watch. New York could not have been a happier place.

Strangely enough, George did not have much to do after his inauguration. Congress began meeting straightaway, but because it had agreed that the legislative powers were to be separate from the executive powers, the president did not meet with Congress as it created and set the rules for various federal departments. When it had decided on what positions were needed, George would then be able to get to work filling them.

In the meantime George had hundreds of smaller decisions to make. There had never been a president of the United States before, and no one could say for sure how he should act, though everyone did seem to have an opinion. One of the first questions people asked George was, What shall we call you? People had many suggestions. Some people started calling him "Your Excellency," while newspapers reported on the inauguration of "His Elective Highness." John Adams, George's vice president, favored "His Highness the President of the United States and the Protector of the Rights of the Same." That was a bit much for George, who wanted something plain and dignified, something that would reflect the democratic nature of the new nation. He settled on "The President of the United States" and "Mr. President" for short.

Now that people knew how to address him, George had to decide how a president should behave. Should he be seen in public or not? Was he able to ride his horse, or should he travel only in a carriage now? And where could he go? Was it necessary for the president to visit each of the states in the union, or should he stay near Congress in case of emergency? Could he go to a friend's house for dinner, or would people think he now "owed" that friend a political favor? Could he have a day off from being president, or was he president even when he was on vacation? Did he need to host official balls and dinners, or would that be a waste of federal money? Should he model himself after a British king, have a palace built, and hold court? Many people thought so. To them, anything less would make the United States look as though it was not important. Others argued that the president was elected to serve the people and he needed to live like them. The questions seemed to go on and on.

George would like to have welcomed everyone who came to the door at Cherry Street, just as he did at Mount Vernon. But so many people came to see him in the first few days there that he realized he would never get any work done if he stopped to talk to them all.

Eventually George and Martha settled on a simple plan, one that they hoped would keep everyone happy—or at least not make anyone too upset! They would hold two afternoon receptions, or "levees," as they were called, each week. Each levee would be an hour long. Martha would also host a tea party for anyone—both men and women—who wanted to come on a Friday night. A small dinner party would take place at 4 P.M. each Wednesday, and people would need an invitation to attend. The Washingtons also agreed that they would not go to other people's homes to visit or eat, though George insisted they would go to public performances at the local theatres when they had the time. Sunday, they agreed, would be strictly a family day. After attending church they would eat lunch and enjoy Nelly and Wash's company for the afternoon.

This new scheme had been in place only a week when George noticed a lump on his thigh. Within days the lump was huge and very painful. Martha called a doctor, who announced it might be a cancerous tumor. More doctors were called, but no one was quite sure what it was. News of the lump quickly spread all over America. Was President Washington going to die? George didn't know, though he was in so much pain that sometimes he thought he must be. Everyone did what they could. Cherry Street was blocked off to traffic so that the rumbling of carriage wheels and the clopping of horses' hooves would not disturb the president.

It was nearly a month before the doctors could say for sure that it was not cancer. They lanced the lump, and very slowly George began to recover.

George still sat with his leg propped up on pillows when, in early August, he read Congress's report on how the new government would be arranged. Congress had created three executive departments, war, state, and treasury, and two federal agencies, headed by an attorney general and a postmaster general. These five represented the goals of the United States government. To protect the nation, the government had to have a war department. To collect taxes to pay for government, it needed a treasury. To have a unified policy in dealing with foreign countries, it needed a department of state. To have a uniform system of justice, it needed an attorney general. And lastly, to join all of the states' various mail systems into one large system, a postmaster general was needed. Over one thousand individual positions had to be filled, and President Washington had to nominate them all.

George braced himself for the onslaught of mail he knew would soon be coming. And come it did. From every part of the United States people wrote to ask for jobs for themselves or for their sons. Men who had been injured in the Revolutionary War reminded George of the debt their country owed them. Women who were widowed by the fighting begged George to employ their sons. Even George's own nephew, Bushrod Washington, wrote asking for the position of United States district attorney in Virginia. But George was determined not to listen to anyone's pleas. As far as he was concerned, the most qualified person should get the job, and that was that. But who were these people?

Some heads of departments, whom Congress named "secretaries" and who would form George's cabinet, were easy to decide on. Henry Knox, for instance, was an obvious choice for Secretary of War. He had always been loyal and dependable and had been in charge of war-related matters in the old Congress. Secretary of the Treasury was an easy choice, too. In George's opinion no one was better suited than Alexander Hamilton, the man who had been his personal aide from 1777 to 1781. Hamilton had gone on and become a shrewd New York lawyer, and that shrewdness was just what the position needed. George knew that this was a key position in the new government because every state would be watching how the federal taxes were collected and where they were spent. The Secretary of the Treasury would have to spend wisely and openly and balance the advantages given to one state with those of the others so that no one got jealous.

George had his eye on John Jay to be Secretary of State, but Jay had his heart set on being a

Supreme Court justice, so George chose Thomas Jefferson for the task. Jefferson was a fine choice because he had spent many years in France. In fact, he was there when he was nominated. He understood European politics as well as anyone could. And this was important because the political situations in Europe were getting more complicated all the time. By all accounts, King George III had gone mad and needed to be constrained in a strait-jacket. As well, Lafayette had just written to George telling him that a revolution was under way in France. Ironically this was partly due to the King of France's support of the American Revolution. France had spent over 250 million dollars helping the Americans, and now the country had run out of money. Like the heads of most governments, the king decided to raise taxes to pay the country's debts. This only inflamed the people and led to chaos. On July 14 the people of Paris attacked the city's ancient prison called the Bastille. They freed the prisoners and forced the nobles to give up their privileges. A revolutionary committee of middle-class citizens was organized, and Lafayette was made commander in chief of the new National Guard, whose job it was to safeguard the revolution. Lafayette finished his letter by telling George that the French people called him *le Washington français*—the French Washington.

George was not sure how he felt about the letter. He wished his young friend well, of course, but he was concerned about what would happen next. He knew from personal experience that there were a lot of potential problems and pitfalls to be overcome in the course of making a new government. He hoped that France could avoid massive bloodshed in the months to come.

For Attorney General, George chose fellow Virginian Edmund Randolph, and Samuel Osgood became Postmaster General.

Just as these nominations were sent to Congress for approval, George received some bad news. His mother, who was eighty-one years old and had been sick for some time, had died on August 25. Now George had to think about how a president should mourn. Once again he decided to keep things simple. He ordered black armbands for his family and his staff to wear, and he canceled the levees at the President's House for a week.

It was not until September that things settled into being "normal" for George. His health was better, the mourning was over, and he had a cabinet in place to work with.

In October Congress was busy working on the Bill of Rights, as it had promised the states it would do. But George had plenty to keep him busy as well. He was a man for detail, especially when it came to making appointments to the various government positions. Not only did he appoint lighthouse keepers at various points along the coastline, but he also negotiated to get the best price on lamp oil. Bigger matters concerned him, too, especially the growing factions in his cabinet.

By 1790 Alexander Hamilton had become the spokesperson for a party who called themselves Federalists, while Thomas Jefferson had become the champion of the Republicans. The Federalists believed that the government should pay the most attention to rich and "well-born" people because they were the natural leaders of the country. Jefferson and the Republicans believed the opposite was true, that the aim of government should be to serve all of the people and that anyone who was good enough should be able to play a role in government. George thought this was ironic because Alexander Hamilton was the son of an unmarried housekeeper while Thomas Jefferson came from a rich and privileged family. Before long the men were arguing publicly, even writing nasty letters about each other in the newspapers. It was all much more of a headache than George had imagined it could be, but he was determined to find a way to keep the government functioning as one unit.

In May 1790 Rhode Island finally ratified the Constitution. Now all thirteen states were in the union.

In July George signed a bill into law that set aside a site on the Potomac River for a "federal city," a permanent capital city for the United States and seat of its government. It was estimated that it would take ten years to plan, lay out, and build the city. In the meantime, it was decided that the government should move from New York back to Philadelphia until the new city was completed.

On September 6, 1790, the Washingtons returned to Mount Vernon for twelve weeks of vacation. George was exhausted from all of the arguing between the Federalists and the Republicans and was glad to get away from government for a break.

Chapter 19

The Greatest Character of the Age

George Washington and his family did not return to New York. By the time their vacation was over, the government had moved to Philadelphia, where George had rented a new home. George hoped for a new start, too, with much less bickering between Hamilton and Jefferson. It was not to be. The two men seemed to disagree on everything, and as time went on, the revolution in France divided not only the U.S. cabinet but also the entire country.

In August 1792 the new government in France declared it would have no more kings and queens. France would be a republic, just like the United States. George began to fear that things in France were going to get a lot worse before they got better. He was right.

Hamilton and Jefferson and their respective parties had opposing ideas on what to do about the upheaval in France. The Federalists opposed the revolution and urged the United States to side with the British and go to war to rescue the old French way of life and bring back the king. The Republicans, on the other hand, wanted to go to war to help the new French government keep control of the country. After all, the people of France had helped America in its time of need.

The whole situation was difficult for George. On a personal level he worried about the Marquis de Lafayette and the many other French officers who had served so loyally under him. But as president he had to try to keep the Republicans and Federalists from tearing the United States apart over the issue.

By the end of his four-year term as president, George was exhausted. Unlike many in the Congress, he had never trained as a lawyer and was not used to endless arguments over trivial matters. He was a soldier and a planter, and he wanted to go home to Mount Vernon. So he told Congress they would need to find a new president—someone else willing to take on the thankless task.

Strangely enough, although Hamilton and Jefferson could agree on nothing else, they both agreed that to lose George Washington as president would be a disaster for the country. They both, along with almost every other person in the country, thought George was the only man who could keep everything and everyone together.

Privately, Hamilton and Jefferson begged George to stay on and submit his name for a second term as president. At first George balked, but eventually he came to think of it as his duty to do so. When he told Martha he had changed his mind and would seek a second term, she did something she rarely ever did. She lost her temper and yelled at her husband! She apologized soon afterward and broke down sobbing. George laid his head on her shoulder, tears wetting his eyes. "My poor Martha," he said.

On February 13, 1793, George Washington was unanimously elected for a second term as president. Once again his vice president was John Adams.

A month after his reelection George received word that King Louis XVI had been executed in January. The king's head had been cut off using a "scientific" new apparatus called a guillotine. The Marquis de Lafayette, who had spoken out against the killing of the king, had fled to Austria, where he was put in prison. Soon after that, Lafayette's wife wrote to George to say she was sending her son, fifteen-year-old George Washington Lafayette, to safety in America. George wrote back immediately and offered to watch over him and pay his tuition at Harvard University.

As it turned out, the execution of the king was just the first among thousands of executions in a period that soon became known as the "Reign of Terror." It seemed that no group of people in France could escape the guillotine. Anyone from nobleman to farm girl, priest, lawyer, doctor, even shoemaker, could be dragged off for a ten-minute "trial" in which a person just had to look scared to be pronounced guilty of a crime against the republic and sentenced to immediate beheading!

Every dispatch that came from France listed the names of more French officers who had served under George that had now been beheaded. George was deeply saddened by each dispatch he received.

The situation in France raised the interesting question of which French government the United States owed its loyalty to. After all, it was King Louis XVI, not the new republic, who had come to America's aid. It seemed that America could not settle on the issue. There were huge demonstrations in the streets, and when George did not push for American troops to go and fight in Europe, some Republicans threatened to drag him from his house and tar and feather him.

By April 22, 1793, George had heard enough bickering over whether to support France or England as the revolution began to spread beyond France's borders. The French army was intent on "liberating all of Europe" and declared, "All governments are our enemies, and all people are our friends."

George did not mind being friends with the French, but there was no way he was going to war with a foreign power on their behalf. He argued that the country did not have enough money to go to war and that its first duty was to keep itself strong. He issued a Proclamation of Neutrality, which stated that the United States would not go to war for any other country unless not doing so threatened America's own peace. It also forbade Americans to take part in any war not declared by Congress.

The proclamation was a good idea, but since the United States had not sided with Britain, the British decided to seize American ships and cargo headed for France and force the sailors aboard these ships to serve in the Royal Navy. In November 1793 alone, the Royal Navy seized 250 American ships bound for France.

The situation got worse. France sent "Citizen" Genêt to the United States to stir up hatred for Britain and the American president who would not come to France's aid. On May 12, 1794, George and Congress sent John Jay to London to demand that the British pay for all the ships and cargo they had seized and, while they were at it, get out of the forts in the Ohio Valley where they still kept troops.

It was not just Europe that was in turmoil, however. That summer hundreds of western Pennsylvania farmers came together to protest the federal tax that had been levied against the whiskey they produced. The farmers used the whiskey as barter, and for many of them it was the only form of currency they had. However, Hamilton had set a tax of 50 percent on their whiskey and demanded that it be paid in U.S. currency. There was no way many of the farmers could pay this tax, so they took matters into their own hands. A mob went on a rampage, burning the tax collector's office.

When George heard about the uprising, he was furious. He saw it as the work of Republicans trying to stir up trouble. Things went from bad to worse, until George felt he had no choice but to show the farmers that the federal government meant business. He ordered thirteen thousand militiamen to march on western Pennsylvania. To make the point very clear, he even put on his general's uniform and hurried off to lead the troops himself.

When the Pennsylvania politicians heard that the president himself was coming to sort matters out, they persuaded the farmers to disband before the troops reached them. Two of the Whiskey Rebellion leaders were arrested, tried for treason, convicted, and sentenced to death. However, once all the fuss died down, George pardoned them both.

Despite the struggles, some good things did happen during George's second term as president. On March 3, 1795, George signed the Treaty of San Lorenzo, in which the Spanish agreed to open up the Mississippi River to American boats and set the boundary between the United States and Florida at the thirty-first parallel. Then, five months later, General Anthony Wayne negotiated the Treaty of Greenville with several Indian nations whereby they ceded much of their land in Ohio and Indiana to the United States government.

On August 18 George signed the treaty John Jay had negotiated with Britain. It wasn't all he had hoped for, but he felt it was better than nothing. In the treaty the English finally promised to leave their western forts, as they had agreed to do in the Treaty of Paris twelve years before. However, the treaty was vague about the British paying the United States for the American ships they had seized. Still, it stabilized American-British relations.

In 1796 three new states, Vermont, Kentucky, and Tennessee, joined the union. Everywhere George went now, he received a sixteen-gun salute instead of thirteen guns.

Slowly, over the seven years George had been in office, the United States had begun to function as a unified country. Not everyone agreed with the decisions that were made, but except for the Whiskey Rebellion, citizens acted responsibly and did not take the law into their own hands. It was just what George Washington had been working so hard to achieve. And now that things seemed to be running smoothly, George announced he would not seek a third term as president. At sixty-four years of age, this time he really was going to retire.

Once Congress was convinced it could not change George's mind, it drew up battle lines for the fierce fight over who would be the next president. Vice President John Adams stood for the Federalist cause, while Thomas Jefferson headed up the Republican camp. The struggle between the two political foes was sometimes vicious, but George was confident that in the end it would all work out and a new president would emerge. After all, the union of states already had eight years of history behind it, and in that time the states had stuck together through some trying circumstances.

George arranged for his farewell speech to the nation to be published in the *American Daily Advertiser* on September 19, 1796.

When the votes for the new president were tallied, John Adams had won by a narrow margin over Thomas Jefferson. This meant the two men would be locked together for the next four years as president and vice president. George was happy about the outcome. He felt it balanced things out because neither side would let the other have too much power.

George watched as John Adams took the oath of office on March 4, 1797. Although he had been to two other inaugurations—both his own—this was the first one he had really enjoyed. George felt lighthearted. Finally the burdens of leading the country were behind him.

When George announced that he was really returning to Mount Vernon to take up life again as a planter, the world gasped. It was one thing for the United States to talk about elections and democracy and the will of the people, but President George Washington had actually stepped down peacefully—and had even congratulated the man who would take his place. For the second time George had done what no other national leader had graciously done before. In 1783 he had stepped down from military power, and now he had stepped down from political power. Even Britain's King George III was stunned. In a rare moment of sanity he pronounced that George Washington's action made him "the greatest character of the age."

Now that George was finally a private citizen again, the only thing that cast a pall over his and

Martha's happiness was the death of George's sister Betty. Only George and his youngest brother, Charles, were left now.

When the Washingtons' coach finally left Philadelphia for home, it held five people—George, Martha, Nelly, and George Washington Lafayette and his tutor. Tobias Lear, George's private secretary, stayed behind to supervise the packing of all the boxes and trunks that were going to be shipped to Alexandria, Virginia, by boat. Wash did not go back to Mount Vernon with George and Martha. He was enrolled in the College of New Jersey at Princeton.

On the way back to Mount Vernon, George took a detour to see how construction of the new federal city, which he had played a big hand in laying out, was coming along. By now people were referring to it as the "City of Washington."

Two things had not changed when George finally arrived back at Mount Vernon. Both the plantation and his finances were in bad shape. No one, it seemed to George, could watch over them with the care he took. George immediately ordered painting and repairs on the house and set about getting the plantation back in shape.

Despite George's desire to retire, duty once again called. In 1798 the relationship between the United States and France deteriorated further. The French wanted the United States to join them in their war against the other European nations. The United States continued to refuse, and at one stage it appeared that France was going to turn on the

United States and attack her. President John Adams asked George if he would once again become military commander in chief. He said that only George Washington could pull the nation through the situation. George did not want to go, but once again he felt that duty left him no option. He roused himself from Mount Vernon and began the familiar process of selecting officers, drafting papers, and attending military parades. Thankfully, the crisis passed and George was able to return home once again.

The year 1799 started on a happy note. Lawrence Lewis, one of George's sister's younger sons, fell in love with Martha's granddaughter Nelly. The wedding date was set for the twenty-second of February, George's sixty-seventh birthday.

Soon after the wedding George decided to write a new will. He had been thinking about what to do with his land and possessions. He left Mount Vernon to Martha for as long as she lived, and then ownership of the property would pass to his nephew Bushrod Washington. He also left things to all his other nieces and nephews, various other relatives, and some of his favorite staff helpers.

But the item that bothered him most was his slaves. Through the years George's attitude toward owning slaves had changed. As a young man he regarded them as nothing more than chattel, something to be bought and sold. But over five thousand black men, both slave and free, had served under him in the war. And for quite some time he had not sold any slaves because he could not bear to break up family groups. Now, in his will he wanted to free them all, but that brought problems with it. Some of the slaves and their children had come to Mount Vernon with Martha, and because of the way her first husband's will was written, these slaves remained a part of the Custis estate. George did not have the power to free them. His slaves and Martha's had married, and George could not imagine freeing some and not others. When Martha died, the Custis slaves would be freed, so George decided to wait to free his slaves until then. That way, when she died, there would be no slaves left on the property. Of course, George hoped they would stay on as farmhands after they were set free.

In dealing with the fate of his own slaves, George knew he was grappling with an issue that his presidency had not resolved, an issue that would not go away with the passing of time. When an Englishman came to visit, George confided in him, "I can clearly foresee that nothing but the rooting out of slavery can save our union."

In September 1799 George got word that his brother Charles had died. He wrote in his journal, "I was the *first*, and now I am the *last*, of my father's children by the second marriage to remain, when I shall be called upon to follow them, is known only to the giver of life."

Six of Martha's seven brothers and sisters were dead by now, too. Even George's nieces and nephews were beginning to die at "respectable" old ages, and only sixteen out of the forty-four born were still alive. Indeed, George had lived many years longer than he ever expected to live.

On December 13, 1799, a steady fall of snow and freezing rain had settled over the Potomac. Three inches of snow lay on the ground at Mount Vernon, and the weather kept George inside for a good part of the day. Finally, by midafternoon the weather had let up enough for George to climb on his horse and take his customary tour of the plantation. When he arrived back, his greatcoat was soaked, as were the clothes beneath. Undeterred, George stayed in his damp clothes and headed for the dinner table,

Later that evening, as George read passages aloud to Martha from the newspaper, he noticed his throat becoming increasingly sore. His voice became raspy, making it difficult for him to keep reading.

"Perhaps you should take some medicine for your throat," Tobias Lear suggested.

"No," George replied, "you know I never take anything for a cold. Let it go as it came." With that he headed to bed. He tossed and turned. In the early hours of the morning, he woke Martha to complain that his sore throat had gotten worse and he was now having trouble breathing. Martha suggested she get up and send for the doctor, but George would not hear of it. The last thing he needed was his wife catching a cold too.

As a wintry dawn broke, the maid came to light the fire in the Washingtons' bedroom. After she was done with the fire, George had her send for the doctor.

Several hours later George's old friend Dr. James Craik arrived at Mount Vernon. He immediately bled George, and when George's condition did not improve, he sent for two more doctors from Alexandria. Together the doctors conferred and agreed that they should bleed George again and give him a purgative to try to force the infection from his body. When this did not work, they bled him a third time. In all George was bled four times that day, but still there was no change in his condition. Indeed, quite the opposite, the combined effect of the bleeding and the purgative had left him weaker than ever.

By now George had accepted the inevitable: he was dying. "I find myself going," he rasped to James Craik in a whisper. "Doctor, I die hard, but I am not afraid to go. My breath cannot last long."

George motioned his private secretary to his bedside. He was worried about being buried alive. In barely audible murmurs he instructed Tobias Lear to wait three days before burying his body in the family vault at Mount Vernon. "Do you understand?" George asked.

"Yes, sir," Tobias replied, fighting back tears.

"'Tis well," George replied.

They were the last words George Washington spoke. Five hours later, at ten in the evening of December 14, 1799, George gasped his last breath. The young nation he had helped to found would now have to find its way forward without him.

Bibliography

Bliven, Jr., Bruce. *The American Revolution.* Random House, 1958.

Cunliffe, Marcus. *George Washington and the Making of a Nation.* Troll Associates, 1966.

Ferling, John E. *The First of Men: A Life of George Washington.* University of Tennessee Press, 1988.

Flexner, James Thomas. *George Washington: The Indispensable Man.* New American Library, 1969.

Freeman, Douglas Southhall. *Washington: An Abridgment in One Volume.* Charles Scribner's Sons, 1968.

Marrin, Albert. *George Washington and the Founding of a Nation.* Dutton Children's Books, 2001.

Meltzer, Milton. *George Washington: And the Birth of Our Nation.* Franklin Watts, 1986.

Randall, Willard Sterne. *George Washington: A Life.* Henry Holt and Company, 1997.

About the Authors

Janet and Geoff Benge are a husband and wife writing team with over sixteen years of writing experience. Janet is a former elementary school teacher. Geoff holds a degree in history. Together they have a passion to make history come alive for a new generation of readers.

Originally from New Zealand, the Benges make their home in the Orlando, Florida, area.